MAN**RAY**

MAN RAY

PHOTOGRAPHY AND ITS DOUBLE

Edited by Emmanuelle de l'Ecotais and Alain Sayag

With essays by :

Jean-Jacques Aillagon

Serge Bramly

Michel Frizot

Floris M. Neusüss and Renate Heyne

Michel Sanouillet

Werner Spies

Lucien Treillard (Interview)

Translated from the French by Deke Dusinberre

from the German by Donna Wiemann

Editor, English language edition Herbert R. Lottman

Laurence King

Exhibition

This book was originally published to coincide with the exhibition,
Man Ray, La Photographie à l'Envers, organized by the
Musée National d'Art Moderne
Centre Georges Pompidou
and held at the Galeries Nationales du Grand Palais in Paris,
from April 29 – June 29, 1998.

Exhibition Curators : Emmanuelle de l'Ecotais and Alain Sayag
Production Manager : Cathy Gicquel
Transport Manager : Delphine Davenier
Exhibition Design : Laurence Fontaine
Framers : Bruno Bourgeois, Sébastien Rodorera
Restorer : Véronique Landy
Photographers : Jacques Faujour, Jean-Claude Planchet, Bertrand Prévost,
Daniel Valet, and Jean-Luc Piété (platinum prints).
Public Relations : Carole Rio, Emmanuelle Toubiana
With assistance from Adriana Loundine and Silvia Labanchi

Book

Photo Selection and Editorial Supervision :
Emmanuelle de l'Ecotais, Alain Sayag, and Gilles Mora
Graphic Design : Ernesto Aparicio, assisted by Caroline Gautier
Editorial Secretary : Claire Marchandise
Copyright : Claudine Guillon and Mathias Battestini
Publicity : Danièle Alers and Anne-Marie Ferrieux

Centre National d'Art et de Culture Georges Pompidou

President : Jean-Jacques Aillagon
General Manager : Guillaume Cerutti
Director, Musée National d'Art Moderne : Werner Spies

Published in Great Britain in 1998 by
Laurence King Publishing, an imprint of Calmann & King Ltd.,
71 Great Russell Street, London WC1B 3BN
Tel   + 44 171 831 6351
Fax + 44 171 831 8356
E-mail calmann_king@compuserve.com

A catalogue record for this book is available from the British Library.

1 85669 150 0

Cover design by Julie von der Ropp

Printed in France

CONTENTS

Calvin Klein

The Man Ray Exhibition was made possible by support from Calvin Klein,

and with the aid of the
Association des Amis du Centre Georges Pompidou.

This exhibition could not have taken place without the help of all those who generously contributed advice or art works. Our acknowledgments go to :

Mme. Nocton, Bibliothèque de l'Institut Poincaré
Marcel Boiteux, Fondation Electricité de France
Mme. Kysslia, Fondazione Marguerite Arp
David Travis, The Art Institute of Chicago
Timothy Baum
Mme. Beaumont-Maillet, Philippe Arbaizar, (Cabinet des Estampes et de la Photographie, Bibliothèque Nationale de France)
Ken Browar
Jane Corkin
Marcel Fleiss, Galerie 1900*2000
Barry Friedman
Sandra Pinto, Galleria Nazionale d'Arte Moderna
Manfred Heiting
Weston J. Naef, The J. Paul Getty Museum
Galerie Kicken
Frank Kolodny
Antony Penrose, Lee Miller Archives
Peter Galassi, The Museum of Modern Art, New York
Gérard Lévy
Harry and Ann Malcolmson
Reinhold Mißelbeck, Museum Ludwig
Sylvio Perlstein
Alain Paviot
Arturo Schwarz
Michael Senft, Jack Banning
Galerie Natalie Seroussi
Roger Thérond
Thomas Walther
as well as to those lenders who wish to remain anonymous.

We would also like to thank Eric and Gregory Browner, Harouth Bezdjian, Jean-Michel Bouhours, Agnès de Bretagne, Nathalie Cattaruzza, Pierre-Henri Carteron, Guy Carrare, Jacques Faujour, Bertrand Prévost, Pierre Ronceray, and Anne-Marie Zucchelli, as well as Serge Lemoine, who supported the estate settlement plan. Thanks also to Jean-Hubert Martin and Germain Viatte, who steadfastly defended Man Ray's oeuvre, and most especially to Lucien Treillard, who constantly made his intimate knowledge of Man Ray's work available to us.

Furthermore, we would like to acknowledge Calvin Klein Incorporated, Calvin Klein Cosmetics, Calvin Klein Underwear, cK Calvin Klein Jeans, Calvin Klein Eyewear, and cK Watches.

Finally, thanks are due to Jean-Pierre Marcie-Rivière, president of the Association des Amis du Centre Georges Pompidou.

"Man Ray, n. masc., synon. de joie, jouer, jouir" *

All attempts to provide an account of Man Ray's immense, versatile production invoke, at one time or another, the definition proposed by Marcel Duchamp : *Man Ray, n. masc., synon. de joie, jouer, jouir.**

There is perhaps no better illustration of this definition than the exhibition presented at the Grand Palais by the Centre National d'Art et de Culture Georges Pompidou as one of the "external" shows being organized in Paris and abroad during renovation work at the center.

Whatever the case, this show adopts an original approach insofar as it aims to present the full spectrum of an oeuvre that constantly stretches and oscillates between commissioned work on the one hand (portraits, fashion pictures, photojournalism), and exploration, speculation, and experimentation on the other.

"I'm not a photographer of nature, but of my own imagination," Man Ray declared in 1951. This exhibition hopes to show that he was, in fact, both. It is precisely this two-way movement that supplied his photographic achievement — shown here for the first time as a whole — with its capacity for formal renewal and its playful, jubilatory power.

The artistic stakes behind the show are matched by cultural and institutional stakes of equal importance. The Musée National d'Art Moderne/Centre de Création Industrielle now boasts a Man Ray collection of unique wealth and variety, thanks to the 1994 estate settlement following the death of Juliet Man Ray (which transferred his archives to the nation in lieu of inheritance taxes), and to the bequest made by Lucien Treillard in 1995.

This exhibition, "Man Ray, Photography Inside Out," is the result of an exhaustive investigation of the Man Ray archives. That task, as documented by this catalogue, represents one of the key roles played by the Centre Georges Pompidou — to enhance and enrich France's national collections of twentieth-century art in a scholarly and historical manner, and to present and share this wealth of material with the widest possible public.

Jean-Jacques Aillagon

President
Centre National d'Art et de Culture Georges Pompidou

---

* Loose translation : noun [masculine] synonymous with joy, jest, exhilarate.

Preface

Visitors who had an opportunity to see Man Ray's darkroom never got over it. They discovered a scene of incredible concoctions. This has prompted me to utter a conclusive judgment : although Walter Benjamin — lauded by historians of photography as the profession's evangelist thanks to two little words, "aura" and "reproducibility" — argued that the question of original prints was meaningless, Man Ray's rich work strikingly refutes that argument. At an early date, Man Ray tried to grant photography a status that would free it from technological obsolescence and repetition, which explains the complicated, singular games of chance that he played in his studio. The effects he obtained from photography are most adequately categorized as surrealist. Man Ray provided his surrealist friends with powerful images capable of demonstrating their ideas and their vision through the medium of photography, whose proof was incontrovertible (at least apparently). The pages of their magazine, *La Révolution Surréaliste*, show that explorers of the nocturnal, invisible realm would turn to Man Ray when seeking plunder. One is struck by his prodigious sensitivity to the epiphany of things, something that could never be repeated. And finally, there is perhaps no finer defense of surrealism's central theme of transgression via eroticism than Man Ray's wanton nudes, who point more to death than to sexuality.

Man Ray once declared that he had never executed a "recent painting," and the same thing could be said of his photographs. He meant that he sought staying power, in contrast to the avant-garde's immediacy and situationism. It was a reaction against the spirit of the times which — unlike Man Ray himself — was more comfortable with instant snapshots.

Werner Spies

Director, Musée National d'Art Moderne

Noire et Blanche, 1926

From One Show to Another *Introduction*

Alain Sayag

Yet another Man Ray show, people will say — and they are right insofar as this is the third exhibition that the Centre Georges Pompidou has devoted to Man Ray since it was founded. The implication is that the number of artists worthy of exhibition is highly limited, or that institutions justify previous choices through a stubborn persistence as simplistic as it is suspect.

Explanations are therefore in order. In earlier shows, Man Ray remained frozen in his standard pose of a brilliant "jack of all trades," a talented dilettante who claimed to do only what he pleased, rejecting all financial and social constraints. This attitude became widely popular, giving rise to an immense cohort of "official artists with patrons, surviving in tepid security, claiming to wield the torch of novelty, boldness, charm, and spontaneity. All that remains of their elusive Marxism is a touching belief that the new remains invincible, that the future is on its side and the wind of history is in its sails." [1]

Man Ray, meanwhile, whatever he may have claimed, was first of all a professional photographer. Thus his work belonged not only to the avant-garde movements of the day but also to the mass culture then emerging. He quickly became a successful *photographer*, as opposed to a successful *artist* like Picasso or Matisse, whose fame and standing were assured by the end of the First World War. No trace remains of his commercial transactions, alas, but the lifestyle he was leading by 1925 attests to the high fees he could charge his clients. Access to the entire collection of 12,000 negatives turned over to the French government by the heirs of Juliet Man Ray, along with Lucien Treillard's generous bequest of another 1,500 negatives that had gone astray — all systematically studied by Emmanuelle de l'Ecotais — has disclosed the extent to which his production was nourished by the tension between everyday commercial activity and the desire to produce "artistic" work. It demonstrates that the hundred or so images selected over time and set apart by Man Ray represent just one side of an achievement of rare complexity.

His selection of images was constantly revised with a view to improvement and reduction, ultimately becoming limited to a few dozen constantly reproduced pictures. Although this reduction effectively promoted his work it disguised its reality, further distorted by another factor, namely Man Ray's adopted pose of amused dilettante, as echoed on every page of his autobiographical *Self Portrait*: "The artist [is] that privileged being who [can] free himself of all social constraint — whose only objectives should be the pursuit of liberty and of pleasure." Several pages later, he even added that he refused to make a film "unless it could be effortless and a pleasure, as making a painting or a photograph had become ...." [2]

Man Ray cultivated this carefree attitude, of course, displaying refined hedonism even in the way he furnished his Rue Férou studio. The bed, which occupied almost the entire space of the "bedroom," was endowed with a plethora of swinging tables that enabled him to carry out his business without ever leaving it. He remained in a horizontal position all day long, like some slothful do-nothing king of yore.

1) Philippe Muray, Exorcismes Spirituels, *Paris : Les Belles Lettres, vol. 1, p. 218.*

2) Man Ray, Self Portrait, *Boston : Little, Brown, 1988, pp. 171 and 177.*

Perhaps La Rochefoucauld was right in thinking that "laziness is the least known of all the passions," that it is "a bliss which consoles every loss." Perhaps it provided the only solace for the loss of the craft of painting, made more complete by the practice of "modern" photography, as though it is better to display laziness or ignorance of the craft, rather than a penchant for a mechanical apparatus.

Man Ray's willing admission of laziness nevertheless reeks of pretense. One need merely flip through the thousands of negatives and contact prints recently acquired by the Musée National d'Art Moderne to realize how difficult it sometimes was to take these pictures, not to mention the task of printing, which was often the object of laborious attention.

There were multiple phases in Man Ray's work. The first concerns the sitting itself. Even though the number of pictures taken was relatively limited, increasing only slightly over time with the change from glass plates to celluloid film, his labor was not restricted to simple mastery of the technical imponderables (such as the aperture/light relationship). Examining, for example, the portrait of Meret Oppenheim, titled *Érotique Voilée* (published in *Minotaure* in 1934, taken in 1933 or 1934), we discover no fewer than nine negatives, showing the patient work of refining the scene. Oppenheim is shown nude, "hands and arms smeared with the black ink of an etching press in Marcoussis's studio." The artist Louis Marcoussis, according to Man Ray, "wore a false beard to hide his identity," but in fact one of these negatives shows him without the bowler and phony whiskers that made him resemble a Landru-type figure. [3] It is the contrast between the ridiculous figure of the malefic petty bourgeois and the vulnerability of the model that make this "very disturbing [photograph] a perfect example of the Surrealist tendency toward scandal." [4]

On other occasions, the final image was honed once the picture had been taken. The artist Max Ernst, who arrived in Paris at roughly the same time as Man Ray, was photographed at least three times in 1935. Man Ray, fascinated by Ernst's "pale eyes and thin beaked nose [that] gave one the impression of a bird, a bird of prey," [5] in fact took just two pictures at each sitting, using a different camera each time. The two first photos, taken frontally and in three-quarter profile, seem to have been eliminated. Of the next two, one was solarized and reworked during printing, as the contact print shows. In the third series, Ernst's torso is placed at a three-quarter angle, but the face is turned to the camera. One of these images was skillfully re-worked: after having made a contact duplicate of the negative through a plate of glass, Man Ray altered the emulsion (by heating?) to create a particularly successful crazed and fuzzy effect.

Many examples of this slow process of maturation could be cited, revealing the extent to which Man Ray's dilettantish pose disguised the work of the professional photographer. If he denounced "craft," and if he stressed chance effects (which he claimed led to his finest breakthroughs, solarization and rayographs), it was simply to emphasize the absolute freedom of the creative artist. It was designed to remind us, in the most elegant way possible, the extent to which photography is just a technique or tool for achieving an artistic goal. Otherwise, photography is at best a record, at worst mere anecdote.

3) Henri Landru was a notorious French criminal who was arrested in 1919 and accused of murdering ten young women. Despite his claims of innocence, he was guillotined in 1922 [Translator's note].

4) Man Ray, Self Portrait (1988), p. 203.

5) Man Ray, Self Portrait (1988), p. 201.

Noire et Blanche, reverse negative print, 1926

Model holding Giacometti's *Objet désagréable*, 1931

DUPLICATING REALITY

The Profession of Photographer

As early as 1921, Man Ray could be described as a "professional" photographer. He was using photography in a standard, utilitarian way — to duplicate reality. First came his "commercial," commissioned work (reproductions of art works, magazine spreads, fashion pictures and portraiture), followed by more personal images that simply reflected reality, such as still lifes and pictures taken during travels. These images offer a different angle on Man Ray's photography, namely the little-known one of the "piecework" photographer. Rather than demystifying his work, they help to explain both its diversity and its rigor. Man Ray's way of making pictures can be understood through study of the cropped contact prints and original negatives shown here full-frame, most of them published for the first time.

Man Ray's "documentary" and "commercial" work appeared extensively in the press at the time, proving that he was highly appreciated for pictures that he later tried to dismiss when he claimed that "photography is not art," by which he meant that artists can not limit themselves merely to duplicating reality.

Tristan Tzara and Jean Cocteau, 1921

Lampshade, 1920

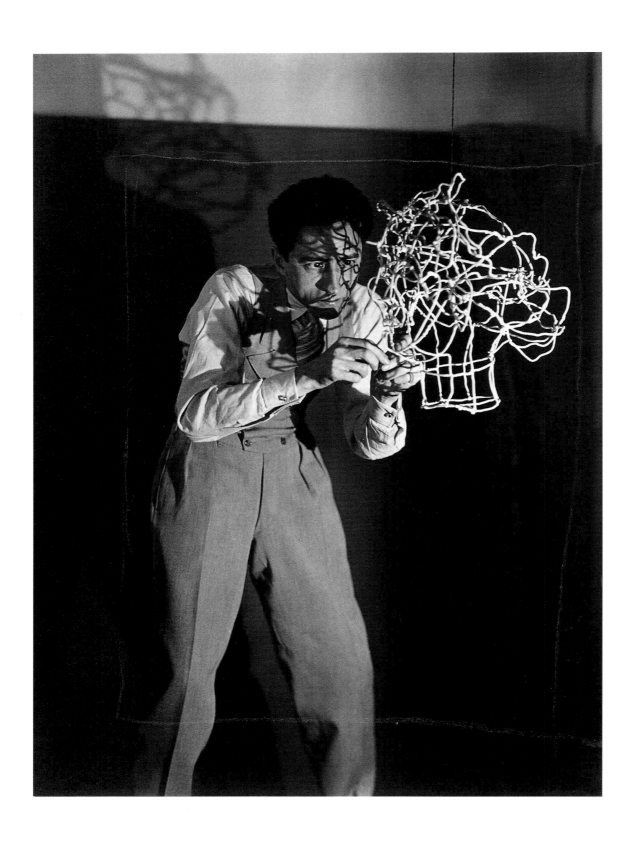

Jean Cocteau sculpting his own head in wire, circa 1925

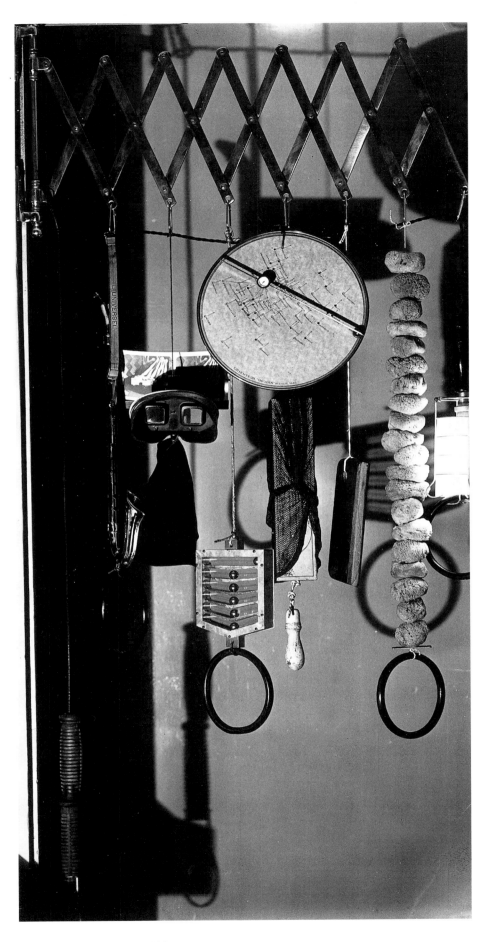

Rideau Diaphane [*Curtain*], 1933

How I Became Man Ray :
The Piecework Photographer   Michel Frizot

The status of photographer is even less stable and codified than that of artist, especially when the individual concerned attempts to balance or combine these two occasionally antagonistic roles by inventing for himself a vaguely hybrid status. Emmanuel Radnitsky was one such individual, and in order to become Man Ray he had to pass from the acquired convictions of painting to the precarious uncertainties of photography via a narrow, initiatory path along which an ancient, noble alchemy was replaced by a coarse concoction of hypo and lenses. And that chemistry of blackness could stain the fingers for a whole lifetime, in such a way that a highly refined artist had to resign himself to working in the photographer's back room, because that was where the work truly materialized.

Man Ray the painter became a photographer only because he needed to preserve a photographic record of his canvases. That, however, is part of the ontological nature of the medium — while people may paint out of desire, out of faith, or out of excitement, they take photographs "in order to" (initially, at least, even if they find better reasons later). People take photographs in order to please someone, in order to perform a given objective task, or in order to disseminate an image designed for a specific function, use, or role. Despite having frequented Stieglitz's gallery in New York, which was mainly devoted to art photography, Man Ray had not been drawn to a medium that, in those days of pictorialism, seemed to flaunt grand airs without really possessing the means. The young Man Ray commented on the way Stieglitz took an impromptu portrait during a visit to the gallery in the following terms : "It lasted about ten seconds." [1] He admired the ease yet lamented the fashionable pointlessness of a personal image. It was certainly not this incident that spurred Man Ray to imitate the master. He was much more enthusiastic, on the other hand, about the idea of obtaining photographic reproductions of his paintings in order to publicize them, keep a record, or provide an illustration. "There was no question of using a camera ... except as a means of recording the [paintings]." [2] He went on to add, probably impressed by Stieglitz's obvious mastery, that "it was much simpler than [he had] imagined." Shortly after separating from his first wife, deciding to face up to the inevitable realities confronting an unknown, penniless artist, he told his new acquaintance Berenice Abbott that he was "taking up photography."

He only really "took it up" when Katherine Dreier, co-founder of the Société Anonyme with Man Ray and Marcel Duchamp, exclaimed, "So, [you're] a photographer." [3] Being a photographer was ultimately the effect of recognition alone, as though technique, practice and title (even usurped) had not sufficed. Dreier, the patron, went on to suggest that Man Ray photograph the works in the society's collection so that they could print "postcards of the works exhibited" which, Man Ray added, "would add to the income." [4] Thus a photographer was born, behind the scenes — as it were — of a desired activity ; the tinkering novice was waiting in the wings for a still-unobtainable artistic role.

1) Man Ray, Self Portrait, Boston : Little, Brown, 1988, p. 26.

2) Man Ray, Self Portrait (1988), p. 55.

3) Man Ray, Self Portrait (1988), p. 78.

4) Man Ray, Self Portrait (1988), p. 78.

Vu, n° 10. 23 May 1928, cover

The Little Review, winter 1926, vol. XI, n° 2, p. 73
The Little Review, winter 1926, vol. XI, n° 2, p. 74

5) *Letter from Man Ray to Katherine Dreier, February 20, 1921*

Man Ray felt he had already been waiting too long when he arrived at Saint-Lazare train station in Paris. He was met by Duchamp and soon joined a merry band of artists even more dubious than him (Tzara, Picabia, Rigaut, Breton, Aragon, Soupault); he was accepted as *dada* (although dada was in full crisis) and as a painter, which mattered little since he was never even asked to prove himself. Instead, he was asked to take photographs, because it seemed he was a photographer — in other words, unique. This individuality was highly useful in the eyes of his new companions, who were little inclined to familiarize themselves with precision mechanics, optics, and chemistry. Most of the photographers associated with the Parisian art scene of the time — Kertész, Krull, Brassaï, Eli Lotar, Berenice Abbott, Lee Miller — were immigrants. Young Frenchmen, more disposed toward poetry and literature, willingly abdicated less noble tasks : photography was perhaps not worthy of a great intellectual calling. Man Ray was therefore the first to benefit from the sincere incompetence of poet friends who left the way clear for him. He benefited all the more since, like other immigrants, he managed to make a substantial living from it (given his inability to craft words, catalogue libraries, recite on stage, or edit ephemeral reviews, as the likes of Breton, Eluard, Crevel, Aragon, Desnos and Tzara would do).

By chance, coincidence, necessity and good fortune, Man Ray was a photographer when he arrived in Paris — or at least, he knew how to take photographs. This role provided him with a back door or service entrance for joining a group of clever, carefree intellectuals, the way a back staircase provides access to a grand mansion. He aimed to use his camera like a typewriter, [5] and so his photography enabled him to shine among those who really knew how to use typewriters. Man Ray thus became official portraitist to these gentlemen, first based in his hotel room on Rue Delambre, then on Rue Campagne-Première, where he soon installed a studio and darkroom. There is no point asking whether he displayed exceptional skill or adaptability — it is in the nature of photography and notably portraiture to respond to demand, to expectations, and ultimately to commissions. And it was in the nature of the demands of his artist and poet friends to choose the carefree, innovating and droll attitude of a dadaist friend over a strait-laced, bourgeois portrait studio (which would have been unthinkable, in fact).

The singularity of the photographer was sometimes due to his status of plodding pieceworker, of someone who knows how to perform simple tasks alien to others (literati completely flummoxed by a screwdriver). In a way, a photographer knows how to marvel at little things, directing his gaze toward insignificant details, never regretting the grandiose inner debates that others indulge in. Photography has thrived on this difference since its beginnings, as recognized by Delacroix and Baudelaire, on its servile yet protective mechanical particularity that keeps evanescent artists at a distance.

Man Ray had no choice but to invent a style for a profession already chosen by his peers — within the Paris art scene of 1921, however, photography was a vacant new field just waiting to be occupied. This was especially true since the professionals — heirs to the major nineteenth-century studios, namely Reutlinger, Paul Nadar, Seeber, Manuel, and Harcourt — had banked on massive adaptation to general public taste, on standardization, on a single style for a chosen class. Given an artistic microcosm easily impressed by common skills and vernacular culture, the best innovation would be to adopt the amateur techniques stemming from the miniaturization of cameras and simplification of processes, something that professionals could never permit themselves. All photographic avant-gardes of the 1920s, whether constructivist or surrealist, relied on self-proclaimed technical competence, on inflated authority and on wariness of professionalism, which resulted in a straightforward, casual technique that until then had been the mark of an amateur. Neither Moholy-Nagy, Rodchenko, Kertész, nor Man Ray attended schools of photography and darkroom technique, nor studied the science of artificial lighting. They acted instinctively, sliding unperturbed into what would be considered, elsewhere, professional errors — (systematic) diagonal framing, visual puns, exaggerated physical features, overlapping images, the blur of movement, and superimposition or double exposure of negatives (Man Ray's 1921 portrait of Tzara). The top of a sitter's skull might be photographed, or the sitter lathered with shaving cream (Duchamp by Man Ray); the photographer need not wait for the sitter to be properly installed, could confine the subject to a fragment of the picture, exaggerate distance or nearness, wield the camera without really aiming it, crop the figure, or abandon the fully equipped studio for private places, everyday situations, and naked eroticism. In every case, this meant subverting the real, calculated, optimal potential of an industrialized system; instead, chance was raised to the level of a creative principle — an avant-garde credo in both literature and photography. Soon, darkroom accidents like rayographs (or photograms) and solarization became a special mark of artistry. It was therefore not surprising that Man Ray, the amateur, provided dada artists and poets with images displaying stylistic rupture, ignoring outmoded constraints and exploiting the freedom of the untrained. Photography, much more than painting, transformed every gesture into a fortuitous throw of the dice, which could only delight those lovers of the poetry of randomness and risk.

It was therefore also natural that Man Ray began to take pictures "in·order to...," that is to say allotted a predefined function to the practice of photography (without excluding later, deflected uses). He took pictures of the work of his painter friends (notably Picabia), and of his own objects (which often disappeared, leaving photographs as the sole record of the work, thereby becoming file records). At the end of a session, he would save one plate for a portrait of the painter, aware of the unavowed narcissism behind the financial imperatives. It was only later that his shot of Duchamp's dusty "Large Glass" — taken purely out of friendship — became *Élevage de Poussière* [Dust Breeding], a work by Man Ray, in a symmetrical but similar relationship to Duchamp's tonsuring of himself, which became an artwork thanks solely to photography.

Yet the photographic portraits not only fed off personal satisfaction and professional schism, they also responded to a need for publicity, in the form of dedicated prints or postcards — the equivalent of todays "p.r." — used for articles in periodicals, the frontispieces of books, the walls of book stores, or shop windows. If Man Ray moved to Rue Campagne-Première in July 1922, it was precisely to handle "the increasing amount of work." *Vanity Fair* was publishing portraits by the "American painter" as early as 1922 (the one of the marquise Casati appeared in October). And if Man Ray became a society portraitist despite himself, it was due to the almost therapeutic nature of the rage for images of oneself; the choice of a practitioner's office partly accounted for the curative effect, as Man Ray

Art et Médecine, October 1931, n.n., p. 20-21
Art et Médecine, October 1931, n.n., p. 30-31

Ballet Russe, *Jack in the Box*, 1926

understood when he stated that people came to him "as though [he] were a doctor."

Man Ray's photographs generally had — at the outset, at least — an assumed goal and destination, and like those by Kertész and Brassaï, they performed an illustrative role. This is witnessed by the extensive publication of his photos not only in *Vanity Fair, Variétés, Vogue*, and *Harper's Bazaar* — great consumers of portraits — but also in *Der Querschnitt, Les Nouvelles Littéraires* and, more surprisingly, *Art et Médecine* (for which Kertész worked) and the racier *Paris Magazine* (where Brassaï's nudes were more likely to be found). Despite his status of painter and artist at the service of the *Révolution Surréaliste*, Man Ray deigned to send pictures to an illustrated weekly like *Vu*, if only on commission (the September 26, 1928, issue announced Man Ray as special correspondent assigned to the steel plants at Saulnes, in Lorraine). Several covers resulted from this collaboration — the dancer Escudero, Miss France, Mademoiselle Dorita the Snake Charmer, and Magda Schneider.

There is probably no mutually exclusive manichaeism in Man Ray's work between bread-and-butter photography (to which he certainly succumbed at certain times) and an essentially artistic and creative achievement. To the contrary, his work extends across various categories, all open to being recycled or deflected into another role or meaning, each feeding off the other, reaching different audiences. What they all shared was the de-sanctified technique of the modest amateur who skillfully seized every opportunity to adapt his approach to his ends.

"Everyone will tell you that I am not a painter. That is true. At the beginning of my career, I at once classified myself among the photometrographers. My works are purely photometric," wrote Man Ray in a 1959 pastiche of Erik Satie's haughty modesty. [6] But his systematic rejection of the label of "photographer" covers only the split with the shameful model of the tame and affluent professional photographers of the 1920s with their main-street studios. Man Ray, as "faultographer," was obliged to assert the simplicity of his origins and the modest, artisanal, and amateur roots of an entire sector of twentieth-century art.

6) Man Ray, *catalogue of the exhibition at the Musée National d'Art Moderne, Paris, 1972, p. 19. English version is reprinted in Man Ray*, Self Portrait *(1988), p. 304.*

25

Antoine, "Le sculpteur de masques", 1933

Antoine, "Le sculpteur de masques", 1933

A head of Buddha, stolen from Angkor by Titaÿna, 1928

Titaÿna, 1928

Mlle Dorita, Charmeuse de Serpents [Snake Charmer], 1930

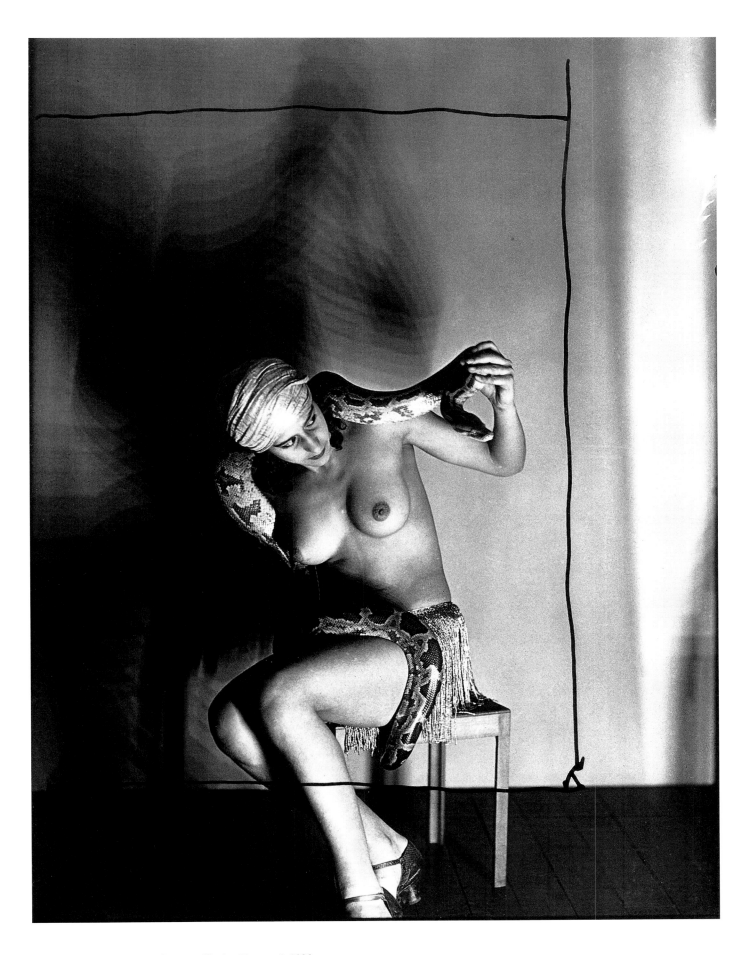

Mlle Dorita, Charmeuse de Serpents [Snake Charmer], 1930

Mlle Dorita, Charmeuse de Serpents [Snake Charmer], 1930

Mlle Dorita, Charmeuse de Serpents [Snake Charmer], 1930

Untitled Advertisement, 1925

Jewelry, for *Harper's Bazaar*, 1935

With its elegant pose and refined setting, the 1936 *Self Portrait as a Fashion Photographer* presents a highly stylish image somewhat in the manner of George Hoyningen-Huene. The irony of the title furthermore suggests that Man Ray was happy to play this role. After all, he enthusiastically produced other self-portraits in costume : animal-tamer, woman, jazz musician, priest, and fakir.

Although this portrait represents just one facet of his work — Man Ray reportedly succumbed to the game of superficial frivolity without ever being taken in — it also reflects the real state of affairs at the time. Whether he liked it or not, Man Ray was a successful commercial photographer whose services were actively solicited on both sides of the Atlantic ; and although fashion and advertising invaded and overwhelmed his existence, they offered fine rewards in exchange — affluence, fame, women. Studio business was so good that Man Ray had his suits made in London, drove a new Voisin car, and bought himself a country house in Saint-Germain-en-Laye. Never again would he earn as much money as he did during the worldwide depression. Yet he was dismayed by these ambivalent circumstances, this particular success, because he desperately wanted to be appreciated for his painting !

So how did he find himself in this situation ? To begin with, imagine a young, ambitious, penniless artist arriving in Paris in the delightful tumult of the post-World War I era. Not speaking a word of French, he pins his future on a few acquaintances made in New York. Not just *any* acquaintances, all the same, for they included Marcel Duchamp and Francis Picabia, the latter having already published Man Ray's early photographic efforts in his review, *391*.

Not a single work was sold at Man Ray's first Paris show at Librarie Six. So how could he keep the dream alive ? "I now turned all my attention to getting myself organized as a professional photographer, getting a studio and installing it to do my work more efficiently. I was going to make money — not wait for recognition that might or might not come." [1]

He wrote that photography initially interested him only as a way to make a living, and that as his resources dwindled, he turned increasingly to this occupation. This confession surfaces as a leitmotif throughout his writings.

He began by making photographic reproductions of his friends' art works, a not very lucrative business that he extended by doing their portraits (out of friendship and to build up a file). Yet he took his first true steps in the world of popular photography in 1922, less than a year after his arrival in Paris, when Picabia's wife, Gabrielle Buffet, introduced him to Paul Poiret, the "fabulous" fashion designer.

Man Ray has described in detail how, thanks to a second-hand camera, a few plates and make-shift lighting (concocted by the concierge), he launched himself in business ; and how, on one occasion, printing his photographs in the bathroom,

1) Man Ray, Self Portrait, Boston : Little, Brown, 1988, p. 100. Unless otherwise specified, all quotations are from this autobiography.

Advertisement for Man Ray's portrait studio, 1935

he discovered the virtues of photograms, which he called "rayographs." Apart from its anecdotal appeal, this tale has the advantage of developing the three main lines of Man Ray's success : a) Display originality (produce, following Poiret's advice, something different from the stuff that ordinary photographers churn out) ; b) Combine fashion and art (say, a gold brocade hobble skirt with a gilded bronze bird sculpted by Brancusi, *Maïastra*) ; c) Fill every image with line, color, substance and, above all, "sex appeal."

Whenever he entered a new, untested field, Man Ray did not grope as someone else might, because he at once discovered unexpected sources of inventiveness in himself. Now he was to outdo himself all the more insofar as fashion houses were a breeding ground for pretty young women. He learned to dance in the same way, driven by a combination of desire, natural brio, and stubbornness.

His career decision was all the shrewder in that photography was just then entering a new era which radically altered and extended its use. Since the 1880s, a series of inventions and technical developments had continually improved the process of mechanical reproduction, to the point that magazines, newspapers, books, and advertising could finally offer vast new perspectives for photography. Printing made mass dissemination possible, and demand grew accordingly.

Fashion imagery, meanwhile, was still wavering between society photo spreads and hand-drawn plates. Although photographs were winning more and more space in women's magazines, and although they were no longer systematically converted into engravings, it was drawings — and the spirit of drawing (of which photographic pictorialism was an incarnation) — that continued to influence both public taste and editorial policy.

"Make your pictures different," Poiret urged Man Ray. His ignorance of the rules of the game immediately enabled Man Ray to bypass the conventional, hieratic, and dully pompous approach. The introduction of a certain spontaneity into his fashion photographs, whether due to inexperience and lack of resources or not, was no less original than his use of art and sex appeal. One need merely look at what was being published at the time.

During this first phase of his career as a commercial photographer, between 1922 and 1934, Man Ray nevertheless operated on several registers. Although he worked simultaneously for *Vu, Paris Magazine, Harper's Bazaar, Jazz, Vogue, Variétés, Art Vivant, Minotaure* and *Femina*, he submitted highly different pictures to each periodical, ranging from portraits to rayographs. His fashion work was only occasional.

The magazines themselves practiced eclecticism in those surrealist days, willingly mixing genres. During the major Art Deco exhibition of 1925, when Man Ray photographed dresses worn by stylized dummies nearly ten feet tall, placed in the garment section of the Pavillon de l'Élégance, his pictures appeared not only in the August issue of the new French *Vogue*, but also on the cover of the July issue of *La Révolution Surréaliste*, the only difference being that the former carried the caption, "And Siegel has created a new approach to the art of fashion dummies," while the latter bore the title, "And war on work," which could be interpreted in various ways. Conversely, *Vanity Fair* was one of the first magazines to publish a page of rayographs in its November 1922 issue ("A New Method of Realizing the Artistic Possibilities of Photography").

Advertising agencies, already in search of the unusual, were similarly interested in the arts. Never had art been so fashionable. McKnight Kauffer had Man Ray work for London's Charnaux Corset Company in the late 1920s, just as, several years later, Kauffer would employ the leading advocate of the American avant-garde, Francis Bruguière.

Man Ray is thus known to have worked on several advertising campaigns, including ones for Wrigley's chewing gum and Pond's cold cream. Not all is known, however. Significantly, although he kept his files more or less in order, Man Ray saved few traces of these various commissions (in Hollywood, during the war, he had to hunt through book stores and clip newspaper pictures in order to constitute a file of past work). Nor does his autobiography place much emphasis on them, mentioning almost no fashion houses, advertising agencies, or women's magazines by name. Man Ray merely skimmed over such things, as though they merited no further attention, whereas today this work no longer seems out of keeping with the rest of his output.

As a fashionable photographer before becoming a fashion photographer, Man Ray led a lonely but creative double existence. On the one hand he was an artist having difficulty making a breakthrough, and on the other he had a brilliant, busy social life stemming from his "bread-and-butter" work.

Yet he hardly complained at the time. According to Duchamp, the term Man Ray was synonymous with "joie, jouer, jouir", which loosely translates as joy, jest, exhilarate. The great hedonist was a fortunate and highly consenting victim of his own success. The French were convinced that he always kept his eye on the ball, and he took advantage of it by accepting proposals to make repeated forays into film and other genres, without becoming attached to a single one.

This versatile creativity nevertheless wound up doing him "more harm than good." In 1929, following the stock market crash, he was seized with a kind of panic. "People were saying I had given up photography for the movies, few sitters presented themselves for portraits. The magazines shunned me ...."

A series of exhibitions featuring his rayographs — in Paris, in Cannes, and at the Julien Levy Gallery in New York in 1932 — eventually re-established his reputation. This time there would be no half-measures: when *Harper's Bazaar* sought his services, he entered into a contractual arrangement with the magazine. From 1934 to 1940, he worked regularly for *Harper's Bazaar*, insidiously becoming a fashion photographer full time.

"I believe that a magazine must have surprises," declared Carmel Snow, the new editor of *Harper's Bazaar*. [2] She handed artistic direction of the magazine to Alexey Brodovitch, a graphic artist of Russian stock, who immigrated to the United States in order to found a department of advertising art at the Philadelphia College of Art. He taught his students to innovate by being "alert for new visions and techniques."

Brodovitch had known Man Ray in Paris. Their collaboration, which had been Brodovitch's idea, began in startling fashion in September 1934 with *Fashion by Radio*, a "photographic impression" of the French fashion shows. Man Ray employed the photogram effect to screen and stylize the model to an extreme, suggesting

2) The World of Carmel Snow, *New York : McGraw-Hill, 1962, p. 100.*

images transmitted by short wave. The following month, a photograph signed by hand like an art work presented the designer Augustabernard's new line by employing a distortion effect emphasizing a "gown [that] billows at the bottom." [3]

These pictures — purified until they gave no more than an overall impression of the garment, and then magnificently enhanced by the layout — appeared extremely experimental. In the fashion realm of the day, one could go no further.

Although much more substantial, Man Ray's subsequent contributions were also much more restrained even if, faithful to his initial principles, they continued to display sex appeal and a range of avant-garde techniques (notably the panoply of his own special effects: solarization, inversion, colorizing, photogram technique, superimposition). His photographs continued to combine art and fashion (as prop or setting, he would successively employ the *Winged Victory of Samothrace*, a Leonardo sketch, white plinths inspired by Brancusi, birds commissioned from Giacometti, even some of his own works such as *A l'Heure de l'Observatoire — Les Amoureux*). [4]

Yet as his mastery of the genre grew, that mastery almost seemed a handicap. He was becoming weary and eventually began to repeat himself. By the time of the Second World War, he was sending *Harper's Bazaar* old images, like the solarized negative of a nude, colored during the printing stage ("Beauty in Ultra-violet," October 1940).

This lassitude affected not only the work itself. When passing through New York after fleeing occupied France in the summer of 1940, he turned down flattering offers on the grounds that he needed a vacation. As soon as news of his return got around, he "was solicited by magazines to go to work at once. Advertising agencies offered [him] a studio and all facilities. [He] begged off, saying that [he] . . . needed a rest for a couple of weeks." He only wanted to retire to Hawaii or Tahiti where, like Gauguin, he could devote himself to painting and live on coconuts.

In fact, he got no further than California. He supplied a few pictures to *Harper's Bazaar* as late as 1944, but no longer bothered with the constraints of fashion imagery. The caption, for which he must have been partly responsible, of a close-up of a face published in November 1942 is revealing in this respect: "Man Ray, who has been painting in Hollywood, returns to his former medium, photography, with this extraordinary study of a woman's face for the beauty issue." [5]

The return was brief. It would seem that the commissioned work he executed throughout the 1930s — the decade he went from artist to fashion photographer — somehow discouraged him from all future photography. Launched in Poiret's fashion house under the aegis of haute couture, his career as photographer thus ended with fashion, as though fashion had underpinned and illuminated it all along. Exhausted by one, he rejected the other. His cameras henceforth stayed in their cases except on rare and very private occasions.

3) Reprinted in John Esten, Man Ray : Bazaar Years, New York : Rizzoli, 1988, p. 2.

4) Similar inspiration was provided by the African mask in Noire et Blanche (French Vogue, May 1926), one of Man Ray's favorite pictures, and Oscar Dominguez's upholstered wheelbarrow (Minotaure, no. 10, 1937).

5) Reprinted in Esten, p. 66.

Composition, 1936

Meret Oppenheim, fashion photo for *Harper's Bazaar*, 1935

Fashion photo, circa 1936

La comtesse de Beauchamp, Vionnet evening gown, 1933

Fashion photo, circa 1930

Untitled fashion photo, circa 1925

Pavillon de l'Élégance, 1925

Nusch au miroir [Nusch with a Mirror], 1935

Nusch au miroir [Nusch with a Mirror], 1935

Fashion photo, circa 1935

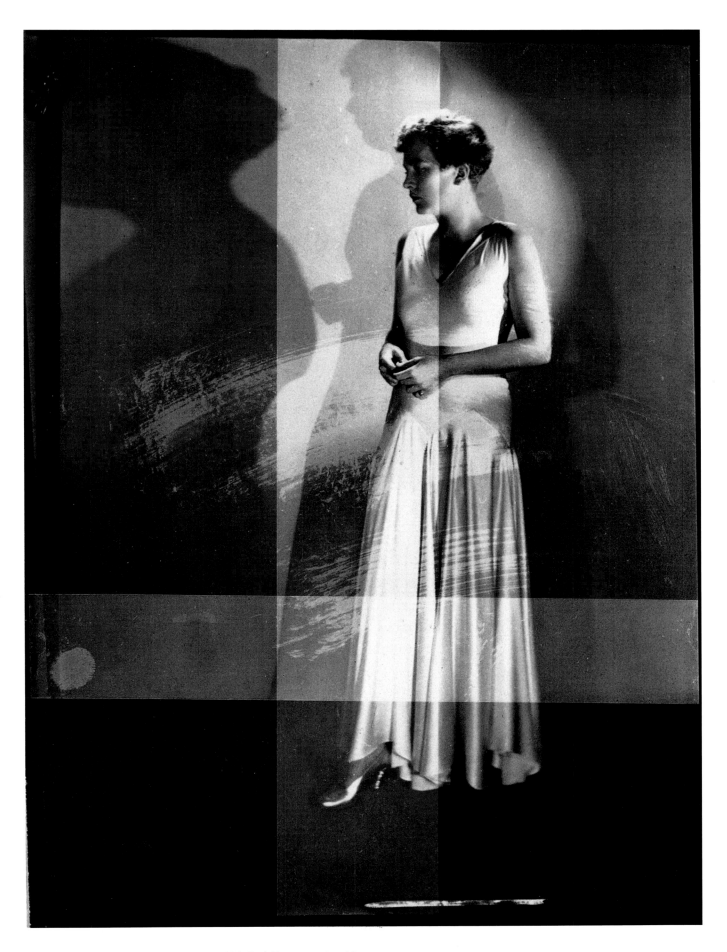

Advertisement for Bergdorf Goodman, 1930. Emily Davies wearing a Vionnet gown

Fashion photo, circa 1935

Fashion photo, circa 1935

From the series *À l'Heure de l'Observatoire, les Amoureux* [*Observatory Time — The Lovers*], 1934

Study for *À l'Heure de l'Observatoire, les Amoureux* [*Observatory Time — The Lovers*], 1932

From the series *À l'Heure de l'Observatoire, les Amoureux* [*Observatory Time — The Lovers*], for *Harper's Bazaar*, 1936

Since Man Ray is now considered to be one of the most important twentieth-century photographers, it is startling to realize that his work has rarely been studied in a "scholarly" manner.

That is what this author now proposes to do, relying principally on the Man Ray estate settlement (i.e., his personal archives of negatives, contact prints, and documents now deposited at the National Museum of Modern Art in Paris, or MNAM), as well as on extensive consultation of periodicals of his time. Such study makes it possible to distinguish between two kinds of work — "commercial" photographs, and more personal, "artistic" work. Beyond the purely formal distinction, however, it is worth stressing the simplistic and restrictive nature of such delineation.

This article will try to show what our examination of the MNAM archives has revealed about the way Man Ray worked, based on examples drawn from "documentary" and portrait photography, his two main sources of income after moving to Paris in July 1921.

DOCUMENTARY PHOTOGRAPHY

Reproducing art works

Man Ray was a self-taught photographer. It is well known that the need for reproductions of the canvases in his first one-man show at the Daniel Gallery in New York in 1915 prompted his purchase of the necessary equipment. "I decided to do something in the way of preparing reproductions of my work for catalogues and the press. The few reproductions that professional photographers had made of some paintings were unsatisfactory. Translating color into black and white required not only technical skill but an understanding as well of the works to be copied. No one, I figured, was better qualified for this work than the painter himself." [2]

By 1917 Man Ray was photographing works for the Société Anonyme, which he founded with Marcel Duchamp and Katherine Dreier. At Dreier's request, he undertook a series of photographs which were subsequently to be sold as postcards by the Société. Dreier felt that Man Ray, as a member of the society, should execute this task without payment, so he was simply reimbursed for expenses incurred.

The negatives and contact prints in the MNAM archives reveal that Man Ray photographed art works by himself and his friends not only on arrival in France but also, more surprisingly, right up to the end of the 1930s. On occasion he even exhibited photographs of his works, notably enlargements of drawings, as happened twice in 1937. [3]

Two letters now in the Lucien Treillard collection demonstrate that André Breton often asked Man Ray to photograph works for reproduction in *Littérature* :

1) Excerpted from Emmanuelle de l'Ecotais, Le Fonds Photographique de la Dation Man Ray, étude et inventaire, *PhD dissertation, Université de Paris IV (Sorbonne), 1997.*

2) Man Ray, Self Portrait, New York : Little, Brown, 1963, p. 56.

3) "Youthful Drawings by Man Ray, 1908–1917," an exhibition at the Galerie Jeanne Bucher in Paris, November 1937, and "E.L.T. Mesens Presents Three Surrealist Painters : Max Ernst, Man Ray, Tanguy," at the Palais des Beaux-Arts in Brussels.

Detail of a
Salvador Dalí painting, *Les Désirs Liquides*, 1932

Paris, December 19, 1922

Dear friend,

It has been agreed that Max Ernst's painting will be brought to my place tomorrow morning. Do you think you could manage to drop by Rue Fontaine with your camera *around noon*? I hope I am not troubling you too much. Only the Picabia and the Duchamp remain to be shot. I don't really know what you can do with the former (*Feuille de Vigne* from the Salon d'Automne). As to the Duchamp, I am still somewhat vexed."

Man Ray executed these commissions for what was probably a modest sum. Breton, for that matter, ended one of his letters by suggesting to Man Ray : "If you have something to publish in *Littérature* (a drawing or something), you know that it will always be very welcome. Perhaps you could send it to me before January 5th?" Man Ray accepted Breton's offer with delight, since the February / March 1923 issue of the magazine published his rayograph titled *Monsieur...., Inventeur Constructeur, 6 Seconds*.

Contact prints in the MNAM archives show that Man Ray photographed Breton's *Rêve-Objet* in 1935 for publication in *Cahiers d'Art*.[4] Such images went unsigned, since their role was purely documentary, which was also the case with a reproduction of Valentine Hugo's painting, *Les Surréalistes*, published in the same issue of *Cahiers*.[5]

An inventory of negatives in the archives reveals that Man Ray also photographed works by other painters including Georges Braque, Giorgio De Chirico,

4) Cahiers d'Art, *no. 5–6, p. 125.*

5) Cahiers d'Art, *no. 5–6, p. 137.*

"*Les os sont à l'extérieur*"
["The Bones are on the Outside"], 1933

"*On pénètre dans les grottes par de tendres portes en foie deveau*"
["The grottoes are entered through soft, calf's liver doors"]1933

Architecture by Antoni Gaudí in Barcelona

6) Man Ray, "*Sur le réalisme photographique,*" Cahiers d'Art, no. 5-6, 1935, p. 120.

7) Spring 1922, vol. VIII, no. 2. p. 41.

8) 1932, no. 8–10, pp. 337–342.

Salvador Dalí, Max Ernst, Jean Hugo, Marie Laurencin, André Masson, Francis Picabia, Pablo Picasso, Henri Rousseau, Yves Tanguy.

He seems to have systematically photographed his own art works, notably all his objects (most of the originals having vanished, this visual material was used to reconstitute those objects in the 1960s, as illustrated in the exhibition catalogue, *Objects of My Affection*).

The "documentary" category also covers some of the photographs that Man Ray produced at the request of magazines such as *Vogue*. Perusal of this publication indeed shows that Man Ray was sometimes required to execute purely commercial work. The French issue of *Vogue* dated December 1924 features several Christmas gift suggestions for "Madame" (a lamp, a tea service), for "Monsieur" (a car blanket, a magazine stand), and for the children (a wireless radio, a breakfast service) — surprisingly, all of these images are signed Man Ray. With only one exception, none of the photos is original in any way. They are purely documentary, simply showing the object for sale. The one exception is the shot of the magazine stand, for which Man Ray employed a soft focus highly inappropriate to this type of advertising. The sole point of the soft focus, however, was to enable Man Ray to underscore the title of a magazine peeking out from the bottom shelf — which of course was none other than *Vogue*, the true subject of the photo. Compared to the other images in the series, this shot is astonishing. One is inclined to think that if Man Ray had not displayed the magazine so visibly, the photograph would have been judged a failure, and never published.

It is nevertheless worth noting that Man Ray had been publishing fashion photographs and portraits in *Vogue* since August of that same year. The pictures of furnishings and gadgets were probably explicit commissions from the magazine. Yet as he wrote in his article, *Sur le réalisme photographique*, "those with the most selfish reasons for profiting from photography — magazines driven by obscurely mercenary motives, which tried to bend me to their needs — … [ultimately] wasted their efforts on me." [6] It would seem that Man Ray produced this kind of imagery for magazines only on very rare occasions.

Man Ray's "Documentary" Eye

Man Ray himself left a crucial indication as to whether or not he considered a photograph an artistic creation. If he signed his photographs, he wanted those works to be recognized as such. When he did not sign — and thanks to archive negatives, contact prints, and other documents we now know which reproductions were his handiwork — he felt he was performing a purely technical task.

When *The Little Review* reproduced Picabia's *L'Oeil Cacodylate*, [7] the photo remained uncredited. When Giacometti's sculptures appeared in *Cahiers d'Art*, on the other hand, they bore Man Ray's mark. [8] Here Man Ray's work was not just a straightforward, faithful reproduction of his surrealist friend's work, since he had endeavored to offer a special vision, which was simultaneously his own and the one Giacometti aspired to convey. Taking the photo of *Pointe à l'oeil* as an example, Yves Bonnefoy has demonstrated how "in Man Ray's photograph, the shadow cast on the figures on the ledge affects in a striking and certainly uncoincidental way the form of this praying mantis who devours her male mate and who so fascinated almost everyone in the avant-garde world at the time. Giacometti placed great importance on photography for the way it represented works by other artists and other periods as well as for the way it displayed his own work; and since he and Man Ray were friends, there is no reason to doubt that this sinister shadow became part of his little sculpture and reinforced its meaning."[9]

Man Ray's collaboration with Marcel Duchamp yielded numerous photographs that could hardly be described as "documentation." When it came to portraits of Rrose Sélavy or to *Élevage de Poussière* ("Dust Breeding," an "aerial" photograph of a section of Duchamp's "Large Glass" in gestation), Man Ray did not limit himself to faithful reproductions of Duchamp's oeuvre.[10]

Nevertheless, a photo like *Élevage de Poussière* seems to have been conceived as a straightforward reproduction of part of *The Bride Stripped Bare by her Bachelors, Even*. Man Ray explained in his *Self Portrait* that he had asked Duchamp's permission to make this picture: "It would be good practice for me, in preparation for the work I was to do for Miss Dreier."[11] The fact that Man Ray and Marcel Duchamp both signed the picture, and that the photograph became another element comprising the Green Box, confirms the fact that *Élevage de Poussière* was above all a photographic record of the development of the "Large Glass."

The image was published for the first time in October 1922 in the fifth issue of *Littérature*, but bore a different title from its current French title (which Man Ray claimed that Duchamp coined much later).[12] The 1922 title read: "Voici le domaine de Rrose Sélavy / Comme il est aride — comme il est fertile — / Comme il est joyeux — Comme il est triste!" [This is the estate of Rrose Sélavy / How arid it is — how fertile it is / How joyous it is — how sad it is!"] It was signed, in French, "Photo taken from an airplane by Man Ray — 1921." This particularly poetic title was probably composed by Man Ray, but it is known that he spoke not a word of French at the time. The only person likely to translate — or even, perhaps, devise — such a title was Paul Eluard. A manuscript exists, for that matter, proving that Eluard translated texts that Man Ray wanted to publish.[13] Although the manuscript post dates the photograph, nothing rules out the possibility that they collaborated as soon as they met.

The original title recurs in a letter that André Breton sent to Man Ray: "Rather than taking the frame off the Duchamp photo ("*Voici le domaine de R.S.*"), I would be delighted if you would supply me with a new print, for which I will pay you, naturally."[14] Image, title, and signature all lent an acrobatic feel to Man Ray's technique,[15] allowing viewers to believe that the geometric pattern beneath the dust represented the boundaries of the fields of Rrose Sélavy's "estate." What was initially designed as practice for Man Ray in recording a work in progress became a work of art in its own right. Man Ray framed it and André Breton wished to buy a print of it.

In 1933, Duchamp advised Salvador Dalí to ask Man Ray to take the photographs for an article by Dalí on Gaudí's architecture, to be published in *Minotaure*.[16] In theory, a photo spread highlighting the features of Gaudí's architectural style constituted a purely documentary exercise. Yet the photographs published in *Minotaure* are signed Man Ray. The two artists truly collaborated on the article, Man Ray's images being considered as important and creative as Dalí's text.

9) Yves Bonnefoy, Alberto Giacometti, Biographie d'une Oeuvre, Paris: Flammarion, 1991, p. 206.

10) Man Ray also performed the task of documentation — the negatives held by the Musée National d'Art Moderne include all his reproductions of works by Marcel Duchamp.

11) Man Ray, Self Portrait (1963), p. 91.

12) Even ten years later, the picture was reproduced in Cahiers d'Art with the caption, "Photograph by Man Ray of the glass composed by Marcel Duchamp from 1917 to 1921, titled The Bride Stripped Bare by her Bachelors, Even. Cahiers d'Art, no. 1–2, 1932, p. 60.

13) This document, currently in Lucien Treillard's collection, is Eluard's translation of a Man Ray article published under the title of "Sur le réalisme photographique" in Cahiers d'Art, no. 5–6, 1935, p. 120.

14) Letter dated December 29, 1922. Lucien Treillard collection.

15) In Self Portrait, Man Ray described how he took a bird's-eye shot of Duchamp's flat panel. Since it was lit by a single, bare bulb, he was obliged to leave the shutter open for an hour (during which time he and Duchamp went out for a meal).

16) Salvador Dali, "De la beauté terrifiante et comestible de l'architecture Modern 'Style," Minotaure, no. 3–4, 1933, pp. 67-76.

Les Arums [Arum Lilies], 1930

Study for *Les Arums* [Arum Lilies], 1930

Les Galets [Pebbles], circa 1933

17) London Bulletin, no. 1, April 1938, p. 17.

18) Janus, Man Ray, Oeuvres 1909–1972, Paris : Celiv, 1990, n.p.

19) Neil Baldwin, Man Ray, An American Artist, New York : Da Capo, p. 102.

20) Baldwin, p. 10.

21) Baldwin, p. 11.

"Holiday Snaps"

MNAM's Man Ray archives include many vacation pictures. It is probable that not all of them were taken by Man Ray — in the 1930s, the surrealists often vacationed together in the south of France, and Man Ray would lend his camera and develop photos taken by his friends. Included among the photographs taken on such occasions are a number of studied, carefully composed images of still lifes (a sunflower, for example, or the shadow of a balustrade). Some of those taken by Man Ray were published, notably in *Photography Is Not Art* (1937). Others, including highly successful portraits like the one of Eluard talking to Picasso, were published with no mention of the photographer. [17]

The part of this series that features card games and swimsuit poses on the beach reflects a vacation atmosphere devoid of originality, except on one point. The difference between surrealists and "ordinary" people probably owed much to the sexual freedom that reigned among the group. A certain amount of swapping and ostentatious debauchery went on — a few of Man Ray's contact prints show a tangle of nude bodies in positions that make it difficult to distinguish who is who.

Some of the photographs that have been classified as "documentation" were taken by Man Ray during boat trips. For example, he took a steep upward shot of the mast and rigging of a sailboat which was subsequently used as the cover of Lise Deharme's magazine, *Le Phare de Neuilly* (1933). Photographs produced in a "documentary" context, then, might subsequently turn out to be "artistic." The advantage of photography over other arts is its swiftness of execution. Man Ray appreciated this swiftness because it enabled him to concretize an idea the instant it came to mind.

PORTRAITS BY MAN RAY, ARTISAN AND ARTIST

Portraits make up the largest part of MNAM's Man Ray collection, giving the lie to a widespread belief that his portraiture was just a "sideline," [18] even though Neil Baldwin long ago stressed the fact that Man Ray not only possessed voluminous "files" but also proudly "claim[ed] to have 'taken' virtually everyone of note in [Paris] or passing through." [19] Until now, however, it has not been possible to verify this claim.

Man Ray liked to promote the idea that his portraiture was purely and simply a commercial affair. It is nevertheless worth recalling that Man Ray had already been enthusiastic about portraits when he was still a young man acquiring an interest in art and hanging out in museums. "Emmanuel was voracious in his appetite for portraits. More than anything else, he wanted to understand the play of light and color upon the contours of the human face." [20] As early as 1910, "he began to take commissions for portraiture in his studio room at home. His first client was a Mrs. Medvedev, who came by only once or twice to pose. . . . He began to dream of becoming a society painter who would do only beautiful ladies." [21]

It is therefore hardly surprising that, beginning with his earliest experiments in photography, Man Ray attempted portraits. It should be stressed that while necessity triggered his photographic career (i.e., the need for reproductions of his

Les Trois Fleurs [Three Flowers], 1931

.

22) Man Ray, Self Portrait (1963), p. 87.

23) This information, taken from Baldwin, p. 71, has not be verified by this author.

24) Alfred Stieglitz founded the Photo-Secession group, which published the periodical Camera Work starting in 1903 and opened the 291 Gallery in 1905.

25) Man Ray, Self Portrait (1963), p. 98.

26) The often-cited arrival date of July 14 is erroneous. See Marcel Duchamp, Ephémerides, Milan : Bompiani, 1993, entry for July 22.

paintings), it was interest and financial gain that spurred his first portraits. His models were his wife, Adon Lacroix, and her daughter, Esther. Man Ray reported in *Self Portrait* that he was "quite pleased" with the results, and that he felt the trade of portrait photographer would not impinge on his work as a painter insofar as his "painting had evolved to a degree where [he] would never consider painting a portrait."[22] Yet money was apparently not the sole motive behind this decision, the proof being the inclusion of a very early portrait — of Berenice Abbott — in an annual photography exhibition. It was Alfred Stieglitz himself, to whom Man Ray had shown the result of his photographic efforts, who advised him to participate in the Fifteenth Annual Exhibition of Photographs in Philadelphia in March 1921. Man Ray's portrait of Abbott was presented under the title of "Portrait of a Sculptor" (catalogue no. 648). He won honorable mention for this photograph, earning him a ten-dollar prize and publication in a local newspaper.[23]

This indicates that Man Ray was interested in portraiture from an *artistic* standpoint right from the start. Otherwise, why show his photographs to Stieglitz (who, more than anyone else at the turn of the century, promoted photography as an art),[24] and why participate in a photography show where only "artistic photographers" exhibited?

Man Ray stated — in *Self Portrait* once again — that while artists, painters, and writers posed for him, he charged no fee, which contradicts his purported desire to make portraiture his money-earner.

It was at this time, moreover, that he began to make a little money ; Katherine Dreier asked him to photograph her collection and to serve as the official photographer of the Société Anonyme. The society also purchased his *Lampshade*, a work he showed at its first exhibition in 1920. Man Ray himself admitted that, for once, his "larder" was full.

Relatively few portraits from that period exist, among them several of Marcel Duchamp (starting in 1916, and as Rrose Sélavy from 1921), a double portrait of Duchamp and Joseph Stella (1920), Edgar Varèse (1920), and Mina Loy and Djuna Barnes (1920). In his autobiography Man Ray described how he sought distraction by inviting people to his studio "as a means of obtaining subjects for portraits. One day it was two handsome young women writers, Mina Loy and Djuna Barnes, the one in light tan clothes of her own design, the other all in black with a veil. They were stunning subjects — I photographed them together and the contrast made a fine picture."[25] MNAM's Man Ray archives contain individual portraits of the two women, but the negative of the double portrait described above has disappeared, as have many pictures from that period.

Working Methods

When he arrived in Paris on July 22, 1921,[26] Man Ray had little or no income. He therefore began photographing the canvases of his painter friends. It was Francis Picabia who encouraged him to pursue such activity, after which a number of artists called on his services. Man Ray stated that he always saved one unexposed plate for the end of the session, in order to do a portrait — uncommissioned — of the artist. He "saved the best for last," as the saying goes, the portrait being done for pleasure.

Studios

Man Ray set up his first studio in the room he occupied in the Grand Hôtel des Ecoles at 15 Rue Delambre in December 1921. Several contact prints in the MNAM archives nevertheless suggest that he produced portraits as soon as he arrived in Paris. Whereas the Rue Delambre studio was already "professionally" equipped (Gertrude Stein's *Autobiography of Alice B. Toklas* records that Man Ray "had three large cameras, he had several kinds of lighting, he had a window screen, and in a little closet he did all his developing" [27]), several portraits in the archives were clearly taken in natural light only, with the aperture opened wide, as indicated by the artist on the contact prints : "F 5-5." These portraits, moreover, lack contrast and are rather dark, suggesting that Man Ray perhaps photographed several (unidentified) people when he was living either at the hotel on Rue de Boulainvilliers or, more probably, in the small servant's room above Marcel Duchamp and Yvonne Chastel's place at 12 Rue de La Condamine. These early portraits represent experiments ; Man Ray noted the f-stop on every image, in order to compare the prints later. Perhaps he was testing a new camera. It is known that Man Ray arrived in Paris with a Graflex as his sole photographic tool. By the end of his life, in contrast, he owned a great number of cameras. It is therefore possible that shortly after his arrival in Paris he had the opportunity to buy or try another one, these contact prints being the results of his tests.

Man Ray's installation of a veritable photo studio coincided with a show of his paintings at Librairie Six, December 3 – 31, 1921, where not a single work was sold. Only then did he realize that he would soon have to find a source of income other than painting. Photography, notably portraiture, which he had already been practicing for several years and for which his services were frequently solicited, seemed like the ideal solution.

Several contact prints in the MNAM archives date from this early period, recognizable by the use of an armchair that must have been part of the hotel furniture, plus a burlap curtain behind the sitter. The room's modest dimensions are indicated by the obvious closeness of photographer and sitter — here the frame never extends much beyond the armchair, whereas in later, improved circumstances Man Ray preferred to maintain greater distance from the person being photographed. Lee Miller commented that he was always at least ten to twelve feet from his sitter. [28] During a 1951 interview with Daniel Masclet, Man Ray stated that he used a long focal distance of 360 millimeters for his 9 x 12 plates — "that way, I can sometimes place myself a long way from my sitter, in order to obtain an absolutely perfect 'drawing,' with which Monsieur Ingres himself could not quibble." [29] He would then crop the face on the contact sheet and enlarge the final print, for he had observed that if he came too close to the face when taking the photograph, the sitter's nose assumed vast proportions in relation to the ears. Man Ray preferred to model the face through lighting rather than through optical distortion. It should also be noted that Stieglitz, who certainly must have acted as adviser during Man Ray's photographic debut, systematically cropped his own prints early in his career. Stieglitz deliberately took his photographs from a distance and subsequently used just part of the negative when printing.

27) Gertrude Stein, The Autobiography of Alice B. Toklas, Harmondsworth : Penguin, 1966, p. 212.

28) "My Man Ray — An Interview with Lee Miller Penrose by Mario Amaya," Art in America, May-June 1975, p. 59.

29) "Man Ray l'enchanteur—Interview de Daniel Masclet," Photo-France, no. 10, November 1951, p. 31.

Man Ray remained in the Rue Delambre hotel for only a few months, from November 1921 to July 1922. Yet that is where he seriously launched his "commercial" activities. Success came swiftly, since within six months the increase in clients justified and permitted investment in a studio. It was also on Rue Delambre that Man Ray discovered the rayograph technique, in late 1921 or early 1922. One rayograph, moreover, is composed of the key to his room, number 37, and a pistol — as though Man Ray, then aged 32, was giving himself five years to make it big or die.

Man Ray photographed the cream of Paris society before he even had his own studio. Usually, he photographed these celebrities in their homes, as was the case with Jean Cocteau (1921), the marquise Casati (winter 1921–1922), and Gertrude Stein (winter 1921–1922). For one thing, he liked to place them in their personal environment, which tended to produce an image of the sitter that was both intimate and "authentic." Further, he was probably embarrassed to receive such "important" people in his modest lodgings. Cocteau and Stein, for example, merited a certain consideration — Cocteau would provide Man Ray with an entrée not only to aristocratic circles, but also to theatrical and musical circles. Stein, meanwhile, introduced Man Ray to her many artist friends whose work she collected, including Georges Braque, Pablo Picasso, and Juan Gris.

With this latter group, Man Ray proceeded differently. As stressed above, he went to their respective studios to photograph their paintings. The contact prints in the MNAM archives nevertheless tend to demonstrate that in the case of Braque, it was the artist that Man Ray wanted to photograph. Then came the writers. It is not known how Man Ray met Sylvia Beach, but whatever the case, he was part of the crowd that filled Adrienne Monnier's bookstore on Rue de l'Odéon on December 7, 1921, to listen to James Joyce give a reading from his forthcoming novel, *Ulysses*. [30] In January 1922, Beach, as Joyce's publisher, sent him to Man Ray to pose for a portrait. Joyce is seen sitting in front of a burlap cloth, apparently uneasy before the camera, giving Man Ray the impression that he was performing a chore. Man Ray went on to photograph many American writers, and the walls of the bookstore Shakespeare and Company were covered with his portraits of Ezra Pound, T. S. Eliot, Winifred Bryher, H.D. (Hilda Doolittle), Marsden Hartley, Kay Boyle, Sinclair Lewis, Ernest Hemingway, Djuna Barnes, Robert McAlmon, Gertrude Stein, and more.

In July 1922, Man Ray moved to 31 bis Rue Campagne-Première, organizing the studio "to receive visitors and handle the increasing amount of work." [31] His business grew. By November 1923, he was in a position to rent several rooms that comprised "a charming little flat" in the Hôtel Istria, 29 Rue Campagne-Première. His studio was henceforth devoted solely to photographic work. In *Self Portrait*, Man Ray commented that it was Kiki who found the new apartment, complete "with heat and a bathroom, which was rare in Paris."

Taking the Picture

The quality of a photograph depends above all on the process of taking the picture. Man Ray managed to obtain a natural pose from his sitters swiftly and simply. Roland Penrose has described a session as follows : "It was as quick and

30) Baldwin, p. 100.

31) Man Ray, Self Portrait (1963), p. 146.

Terrain Vague [*Waste Land*], 1932

Study for *Terrain Vague* [*Waste Land*], 1932

Study for *Terrain Vague* [*Waste Land*], 1932

Nusch Eluard, circa 1935

32) Baldwin, p. 101.

33) "Man Ray l'enchanteur...", p. 32.

34) Meret Oppenheim interviewed by Billy Klüver and Jill Krauskopf, December 11, 1979, Lucien Treillard Collection.

35) André Breton, "The Visages of the Woman," Photographs by Man Ray 1920 Paris 1934, trans. anon., Hartford, Conn: James Thrall Soby, 1934. Dover reprint, New York, 1979, between pp. 42/43.

36) Man Ray, personal notes contained in the MNAM archives.

37) Robert Desnos, "Man Ray ou 'vous pouvez courir'," original typescript preserved at the Fonds Doucet. The text was first published in Paris-Journal on December 13, 1924, p. 5, then translated into English by Maria McD. Jolas and published as "The Work of Man Ray" in transition, no. 15, February 1929, pp. 264-266, from which this and following quotations are drawn.

38) Philippe Soupault, Mémoires de l'Oubli, 1923–1926, Paris: Lachenal & Ritter, 1986, pp. 29–30.

casual as bantering with him in a café. All he used to say was, 'Show your teeth'... he didn't fiddle forever with the lens or the lights." [32] Man Ray himself confirmed this approach in his interview with Daniel Masclet. "Don't tire your sitter, do everything quickly, in ten minutes, don't make it seem like work." [33] In fact, Man Ray prepared all his equipment (lighting, background, camera) before his "client" arrived.

A certain interventionism nevertheless emerges from Meret Oppenheim's account: "He didn't start shooting right away. He knew what he wanted — he'd say, 'Sit there,' and then he'd set up reflectors, umbrella, lights. 'Turn this way or that way... Moisten your lips... Open your eyes.' (Just before taking a picture, he asked you to close your eyes so that they seemed natural when you opened them....) Then he changed the lights, and so on, all before taking any photos.... Above all, he was interested in the lighting. He was very professional. He had a precise idea of what he wanted. When he worked, his movements were paced... he worked calmly and spoke little, except to ask you to shift your pose, and so forth." [34]

As Breton pointed out, Man Ray had "the eye of a great hunter, the patience, the sense of the moment pathetically right when a balance, transient besides, occurred in the expression of a face, between dream and action." [35] Surprisingly, the MNAM archives reveal that Man Ray was not a "machine-gunning" photographer — he took just a few shots during any given session. The number of images per sitter varies from two to 12, with a quantitative increase that corresponds to his growing success. By the late 1920s, clients were regularly entitled to a dozen shots, which is hardly excessive, reflecting Man Ray's comment that "if photographers wasted less film, they might perhaps think less of breaking even, and more of Art." [36]

Like Breton, Robert Desnos described Man Ray's "power" of capturing that moment between consciousness and unconsciousness. "He arrives between two shocks of an earthquake, stops creation on the peak of a plunge, immediately before the return to the normal position. He catches faces at that fugitive moment between two expressions. Life is not present in his pictures and still there is nothing dead about them. There is a pause, a stop, only: Man Ray is the painter of the syncope." [37]

It is significant that it was Desnos who provided this "definition" of Man Ray. The moment between life and death as represented by a "syncope," that is to say a faint or temporary black-out, is related to surrealist experimentation. When it came to their notorious occult seances, which they called "sleep experiments," Desnos was the most amazing participant. Philippe Soupault described how, one evening, Desnos "fell into a sleep [and] began to prophesy. He was highly excited, feverish even, beside himself. He spoke uninterruptedly, and seizing a pencil began to write phrases and puns ...." [38] Man Ray did not participate in these encounters, but they were well known. Moreover, he had a number of people pose first with their eyes closed, then open (Kay Boyle in 1934, Nusch Eluard in 1935), as though he wanted to "reveal" them in that instant of unconsciousness. Desnos explained how, as "a photographer, Man Ray derives neither from artistic deformation, nor from the servile reproduction of 'nature.' Your planes and humps will reveal to you a person you do not know, and whom you have never dared glimpse in your dreams. A new 'you' will spring from the delicate hands of the

Nusch Eluard, circa 1935

chemist in the red glow of the [darkroom]. It will bat its eyes out in the open air, the way night birds do." [39]

In his typically provocative manner, Man Ray explained his working method to Daniel Masclet. "First of all, little in the way of commercial smiles! If you look at a portrait for a long time (you know, of the 'now smile' variety), the smile soon becomes a nightmarish grin .... Naturalness? It's the height of artifice! I give all the orders, directing everything in the studio, I don't leave anything to the client's wishes. Why? It couldn't be simpler : the client knows absolutely nothing about it, since he has only been photographed twice in his life, whereas I study photography every day. So it's obvious that my opinion should prevail. This is the only method that has produced good results, but ... sometimes it takes years of study to know how to *recreate* naturalness." [40] Indeed, the MNAM archives confirm that Man Ray never instructed his clients to smile. There is even one series in which the only picture showing the young woman with a smile is crossed out.

Half-length oil portraits sometimes presented a "problem" for both artists and sitters in that the latter, not completely at ease, did not know what to do with their hands. In order to lend their sitters greater composure, painters (usually) gave gloves to men and a fan to women. As Walter Benjamin noted as early as 1931 in his "*Short History of Photography*," photographic portraiture was not only influenced by painting, but also by the constraints of the young medium of photography. "The accessories of such portraits ... still recall the time when, due to the long exposure, the subject required supports in order to remain still." Although head braces and supports sufficed at first, famous paintings and a desire to look "artistic" soon spurred the use of other accessories. First of all came columns and curtains. The most enlightened critics denounced these abuses as early as the 1860s. Thus a specialized English review pointed out that whereas a column retained an appearance of authenticity in a painting, in a photograph it seemed absurd because it was usually set on a carpet. Yet no one believed that a column of marble or stone had a carpet for a base. [41]

Column and curtain are props that recur in the work of Man Ray. There is one major difference, however : instead of a marble column, he used a wine-press screw; rather than a superb velvet curtain, he used a plain burlap cloth. Furthermore, Man Ray's range of props was more extensive and more original. Above all, these props played an additional role — they gave his photographs a second meaning, or at least planted the seeds of additional significance, opening a window onto Man Ray's own imaginative realm.

One of Man Ray's frequently recurring props is a life-sized hand, or rather forearm, of dark wood, which he especially liked his female sitters to hold. These women — whether anonymous or known, such as Lise Deharme — present the forearm in various ways : placed vertically on a table, parallel to the bust, like the hand of justice (*Lise Deharme as Queen of Spades*, 1935); the palm of the wooden hand placed against the woman's cheek in a natural gesture, as though it were her own hand (itself hidden underneath a shawl); or held perpendicularly to the face, wooden fingers pointing at the temple. Jean-Charles Worth, posing bare-chested, placed the hand in front of his face, partly hiding it. This wooden hand, also seen in photographs of jewelry published in *Harper's Bazaar* (1935), probably came from a clothes dummy. The partial replacement of the human body by a

39) *Desnos, p. 265.*

40) *"Man Ray l'enchanteur...," p. 31.*

41) *Walter Benjamin, "A Short History of Photography," trans. Stanley Mitchell, Screen, vol. 13, no. 1, Spring 1972, p. 18.*

George Antheil, 1924

piece of wood denies photographic portraiture the realism normally expected of it.

Other props recur in Man Ray's portraits, notably the neck of a cello (nicknamed "Emak Bakia") on which he himself leaned in a self-portrait and which appears in several portraits of Jacqueline Goddard. Man Ray also used a simple stick of wood (a series of poses with Luis Buñuel shows how he employed it as a veritable compositional device). In both cases, however, it should be noted that the prop served the same function as head-braces in the previous century.

Man Ray's own musical instrument, the banjo, appears in a certain number of photographs. The portrait of Ernest Hemingway is the best-known example, but others exist, such as the singer Yvonne George, Juan Gris, and Kiki. Most of these portraits predate 1925. The banjo, usually independent of the sitter, is part of the background composition, a round shape recalling the sitter's head. In the case of Yvonne George, the musical instrument also functions as a reference to her profession.

As mentioned above, one of the most famous of Man Ray's portrait props was a press screw. The most celebrated use, of course, was for the portrait of Sinclair Lewis (1926), but the object recurs in portraits of Lucien Vogel (c. 1928) and the Spanish dancer Rolanda (c. 1928), among others. Just as in oil portraits, the column plays a compositional role here. Yet it is also tempting to ascribe a meaning to it — surely Man Ray used the press screw precisely because it related to his sitter in some way. Indeed, when Sinclair Lewis arrived in Man Ray's studio, he was drunk and thus his head was "spinning" (*le vis*, French for "screw," is perhaps a pun on Lewis). Lucien Vogel, meanwhile, "pressed" Man Ray for commissioned work for his magazine, *Vu*. And the Spanish dancer Rolanda would constantly spin while dancing, thereby turning the heads of her audience.

The use of various props furthermore proves that Man Ray composed his images with a great deal of care when it came to details and construction. His training as a painter played a key role here, and the influence of classical painting, visible for that matter in other aspects of his photography, is related to this way of working. Other examples of that influence exist : it is worth noting that Man Ray's portraits often incorporate a checkerboard pattern (which, when it comes to Man Ray, might be called a chessboard pattern), either as a backdrop (*George Antheil*, 1924), as a rug for full-length portraits (*Peggy Guggenheim*, 1925), or as a tablecloth for a half-length photograph (with the sitter's elbows on the table). The checkered floor evokes old masters who painted marble flooring in order to create perspective, although Man Ray was not seeking that effect when he used the pattern. Rather, he wanted to demonstrate his determination to produce a highly composed image orchestrated by what is the very essence of photography — contrasts in light, which are stronger than ever in black and white.

Man Ray's "do-it-yourself" approach is perceptible in many contact prints (whereas final, cropped prints exclude the paraphernalia required to produce the image). He clearly used everything at hand to produce a "good" portrait. He did not hesitate, for instance, to make a client sit on a trunk if necessary, or to use a camera tripod as an armrest.

There was nothing extraordinary about the furnishings in Man Ray's studio in the early 1920s — a simple upholstered armchair, a Biedermeier chair, and one of the gilded chairs commonly used by haute couture houses for guests at fashion

George Antheil, 1924

shows. Later, Man Ray would employ all kinds of wooden chests of varying heights, on which clients would lean or place an elbow, whether seated or standing. Using these chests meant that nothing inhibited the sitter's movements or crowded the image. And on certain occasions they could even serve as an integral part of the composition, as seen in a double portrait of Gala and Dalí (1936). By the late 1920s, the studio also boasted an armchair that Man Ray made himself. Only rarely did he use it in portraits, however, one of the sole examples being that of Balthus.

Man Ray and his assistants : darkroom work.

In the spring of 1923, Berenice Abbott knocked on Man Ray's door, in search of work. According to Neil Baldwin, Man Ray already had an assistant, a young man who "thought he knew everything" and therefore created problems. Abbott meanwhile, had everything to learn, and Man Ray hired her.

The darkroom upstairs was where, "for 15 francs a day, Berenice Abbott spent long hours 'doing everything after Man Ray took his picture' — [such as] developing and printing, which she learned quickly during just a few weeks of practice under Man Ray's subtle teaching-by-doing instruction." [42]

Starting early in 1923, then, Man Ray's assistants performed a fairly complete range of tasks ; from developing negatives to printing the final results, they followed instructions given by the artist. Man Ray thereby delegated a large part of the darkroom work at an early date. He took the pictures, which he then passed on to his assistant for developing. He was very meticulous, however, and his contacts, which he printed himself, bore notations concerning cropping (noted in pencil or ink, although sometimes the contacts were even folded [43]), the dimensions of the print, the type of paper, the contrasts to be brought out, and so on. His eye was so precise and surgical that his assistants had merely to execute the "master's" instructions. Man Ray's appetite for work nevertheless remained enormous. Baldwin even claims that he had an "an antipathy to idleness." [44] As a child raised in modest circumstances, he saw his parents work themselves to the bone. And the number of portraits he produced demonstrates that his studio was always busy. Thus it appears unlikely that the artist abandoned all darkroom work. He probably doubled up on darkroom sessions with his assistant. This does not exclude the possibility that Man Ray occasionally allowed his assistant to take the photographs of lesser clients. According to Lucien Treillard, when Man Ray found himself in the Basque country, he asked Jacques-André Boiffard (his assistant from 1924 to 1929) to handle one (or several) sittings.

The question of cropping is primordial to Man Ray's work. At first sight it would seem that he only thought about the final framing once the photograph had been taken, on studying the contact print, for the sole purpose of *composing* the image. Certain works, however — and not always portraits — reveal to the contrary that he already had an accurate idea of the ultimate frame he intended, proving that the goal of the operation was also to produce a grainier image. The almost total absence of sharpness produced a quality of softness in prints, often done on textured paper, that typifies Man Ray's oeuvre.

This was the case, for example, in the photograph of a nude seen from the

42) Baldwin, 115.

43) It might be added that Man Ray occasionally marked cropping indications on the negative, using the storage pouch to avoid defacing the original.

44) Baldwin, p. 103.

Madeleine Turban, circa 1925

Madeleine Turban, circa 1925

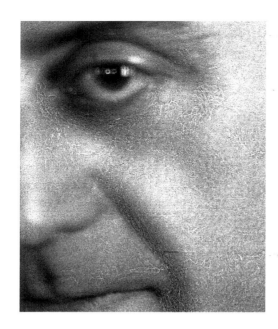

Detail from a self-portrait, circa 1930

back, commonly called *Dos Blanc* ("White Back"), published in James Thrall Soby's album in 1934. [45] The negative shows, on the one hand, that the model was kneeling (not apparent in the print) and that, on the other hand, her knees rested on a cushion for greater comfort. Since it seems obvious here that Man Ray never intended to show the model kneeling — had that been the case, he would have removed the cushion, which is pointless and even detrimental to the image — it can be concluded that right from the start he knew exactly how he was going to crop the image.

Retouching [46]

Man Ray practiced photographic portraiture differently from his contemporaries. They wanted to produce images that were sharp and pure, free from any touching up, often taken in close-up or from a particular angle. Man Ray, however, did not subject himself to any rule. In 1951 he told Daniel Masclet that he almost never did any touching up. "Retouching? I do it as little as possible, that is to say almost never...! That should be left to ... photographers who are unable to sell a portrait without retouching it." [47] Here Man Ray was not being candid, for the MNAM archives prove the contrary: not only did Man Ray frequently touch up his negatives, but he did it especially for portraits, including self-portraits. At the time, however, retouching was considered shameful. Walter Benjamin even claimed in his 1931 *Short History of Photography* that when "the practice of touching up the negative became widespread (the bad painter's revenge on photography), a sharp decline in taste set in." [48]

Note, however, that the practice existed right from the birth of photography, since even paper negatives were retouched.

Retouching was done in pencil on the emulsion side of the plate, usually to eliminate wrinkles and minor skin blemishes. One of Man Ray's self-portraits is completely retouched — the face is literally furrowed with pencil lines. [49] The lines vary in heaviness, being light on the forehead but heavier under the eyes and around the mouth — a veritable face-lift! The delicateness of this retouching work (done with the aid of a magnifying glass) reveals Man Ray's exceptional deftness.

Although negatives in the MNAM archives occasionally contain retouching done in pencil directly on the emulsion, most of the time Man Ray first covered the entire negative with a greasy medium composed of gum and turpentine. Custom dictated that this substance be applied with an old cloth, using a circular motion from the center outward. But Man Ray flaunted custom, usually ignoring this principle by roughly plastering the product over his plates. His lack of interest in the technique can be explained by the fact that the effect remained absolutely invisible on the print. Usually Man Ray applied the substance only to the oval of the face. Remarkably, if unwittingly on Man Ray's part, this medium protected the emulsion from the air and spared the negatives from the chemical degradation of silver salts.

Although touching up was usually done to hide blemishes, it could also be an additive designed to modify the original model. This was the case, for instance, in a

45) Photographs by Man Ray 1920 Paris 1934, *Hartford, Conn: James Thrall Soby, 1934. Dover reprint, New York, 1979, p. 27.*

46) The author would particularly like to thank M. Ronceray for his valuable technical explanations.

47) "Man Ray l'enchanteur," p. 31.

48) Benjamin, p. 18. André Gunthert's French translation of Benjamin's text ("Une Petite Histoire de la Photographie," Etudes Photographiques, no. 1, November 1996) nevertheless stresses in a footnote that, "In fact, the theory of the increase in retouching as a sign of photographic decadence... is clearly devoid of historical basis, and stems from the old curse that strikes the practice — ever shameful, but ever present — of manual intervention on the photographic subjectile." Benjamin, p. 33, note 34.

49) Negatives AM 1995–281 (74), (75), and 76 from the Lucien Treillard Bequest.

50) Daniel Masclet's "Man Ray l'enchanteur," p. 26, quotes Man Ray as saying : "I don't know what a 'good' photo is. Unless it's one I like. (But I don't think a photo is bad simply because I don't like it.) To produce an authentic photo…. "

51) "Man Ray l'enchanteur," p. 32.

nude image of Kiki. As Man Ray mentioned in *Self Portrait*, Kiki was distressed because she had no pubic hair. The artist remedied this situation by sketching it on the plate — the lines of black pencil are drawn in such a fashion that when printed, the area seems marked by shadow and light. It was more a question of discreet effect than of veritable drawing, for that matter.

Man Ray employed other retouching techniques, which entailed removing emulsion. The surface is scraped away to create a hole of light in the image (which becomes a black hole on printing). Man Ray etched the emulsion with the aid of a sewing machine needle with a beveled point. One of the most interesting examples in the MNAM archives is a negative taken when Man Ray visited the count and countess de Noailles in Hyères. After photographing their villa — designed by Robert Mallet-Stevens — he cut away part of the emulsion on the triangular flag flying from the roof.

It was also in this series, taken when he was making the film *Mystères du château de Dé* in 1929, that another negative was retouched with red chalk powder. Once again it was a photograph of the villa, but this time Man Ray wanted to give greater density to the sky by depicting clouds. This retouching was done, however, on the material substrate, that is to say on the glass side of the plate.

Man Ray thus violated one of the basic laws of what has been called "the new photography," which held that photographs should remain "pure." Instead, he worked as nineteenth-century photographers might have, or even neighbourhood studio portraitists. Yet he won almost instant recognition as an avant-garde photographer, and he participated in international exhibitions such as the *Film und Foto* show in Stuttgart in 1929. One of the reasons for his "popularity" is that Man Ray did not disclose his methods. He did so much later, but even then, as already noted, he was capable of lying. He thought that any means justified the ends when it came to a "good" photograph, or rather an "authentic" photograph. [50]

Thus he also employed over-exposure. "I often over-expose my portraits by a factor of three or four — the outcome is very soft on the face. I don't mean that I employ long exposure times. A hundredth of a second can be over-exposed threefold or more ; it depends on the amount of given luminosity … [.] Just as I usually expose longer than other photographers, so I use blacks much less, the latter often being the consequence of the former. That's because, you see, too many photographers naively think that it's the blacks — "rich blacks," they say — that lend strength. In reality, blacks no more give vigor to a photo than "strong" drinks give a man strength ! So I've never added alcohol to my pictures." [51]

Untitled, circa 1930

Kiki, circa 1924

Kiki, circa 1924

Étienne de Beaumont, 1925

Étienne de Beaumont, 1925

Jacqueline Goddard, 1932

Jacqueline Goddard, 1932

Yves Tanguy, 1936

Yves Tanguy, 1936

Nancy Cunard, 1926

Nancy Cunard, 1926

Jacqueline Goddard, 1932

Jacqueline Goddard, 1932

Salvador Dalí, 1929

Salvador Dalí, 1929

La Lune Brille sur l'île de Nias, circa 1924

Portrait of a woman with *La Lune Brille sur l'île de Nias*, circa 1924

Jean-Charles Worth, circa 1925

Untitled, circa 1935

Blanc et Noir [White and Black], circa 1929

Blanc et Noir [White and Black], circa 1929

Chevelures [Hair], 1937

Kiki, circa 1925

Le Baiser [The Kiss], circa 1932

Ady and Nusch, 1937

Lee Miller, circa 1930

Lee Miller [Breasts], circa 1930

Lee Miller, circa 1930

Lee Miller, circa 1930

Meret Oppenheim, 1933

Self-Portrait with Meret Oppenheim, 1933   Self-Portrait with Meret Oppenheim, 1933

Suzy Solidor, 1929

Suzy Solidor, 1929

Nude, circa 1935

DELINEATING REALITY

Photographic Creativity

Alongside his everyday "commercial" work, Man Ray did his utmost
to break the frame of conventional photography. His photographic
"tinkering" and manipulations led to (re)discoveries such as rayographs in
1922 and solarization in 1929. He also implemented a range of effects like
superimposition (of two exposures or of a screen over the negative),
deformation created by moving the paper during printing, inversion of values,
and more. He created illusion through props such as the drops of glass
that he stuck below the eyes of the sitter in *Larmes* [*Tears*]. He constructed,
composed, envisaged and invented a different photography, namely a
surrealist one : pictures were veiled, blurry, or printed in negative ; the outlines
of the sitter were electrified ; back became front, shadow overtook light.
All means were justified in attaining his end — to delineate reality. There
were no rules, no taboos, just the pleasure of playing with the very essence
of photography. Creativity began where reproduction ended.

Kiki, circa 1926

Kiki, 1926

Edward James, 1937

Edward James, 1937

Marcel Duchamp, 1930

Untitled, circa 1930

1) Excerpted from Emmanuelle de l'Ecotais, Le Fonds Photographique de la Dation Man Ray, étude et inventaire, PhD dissertation, Université de Paris IV (Sorbonne), 1997.

2) Pierre Vaisse, "Portrait de société, anonymat et célébrité," in Michel Frizot (ed), Nouvelle Histoire de la Photographie, Paris : Bordas–Adam Biro, 1994, p. 499.

3) Vaisse, p. 499.

4) The practice of copying photographs has existed since the dawn of the medium. In Nouvelle Histoire de la Photographie, p. 361, Pierre Albert and Gilles Feyel stress that the first engraved copy of a daguerreotype was published in L'Illustration in 1848, while the first copy of a paper photograph appeared in 1853.

5) June 1922, p. 7.

6) July 1922, p. 76.

7) July 1922, p. 76.

8) August 1922, p. 72.

9) May 1923, p. 74.

10) May 1925, p. 75.

11) July 1926, p. 70.

12) May 1927, p. 79.

13) April 1930, p. 72

14) October 1922, p. 46.

Art and Portraiture

Emmanuelle de l'Ecotais [1]

The Impact of Illustrated Magazines

The expansion of Man Ray's portrait business owes a great deal to the rise of illustrated magazines. It is worth recalling that magazines were only just beginning to reproduce photographs at that time. It was the "discovery of photoengraving techniques that could finally be used for illustrating books and periodicals" which spurred a "new and massive demand" just after the First World War. [2] And "the launching of magazines specializing in high society, fashion, and entertainment — such as *Vogue, Vanity Fair*, and *Harper's Bazaar* — had a profound influence on portraiture." [3] It should be added, however, that the cost of paper prevented many magazines from taking advantage of the new process, which required a high quality paper that only lavish reviews could afford. As a consequence, in the early 1920s, weeklies such as *Paris-Journal* were still using more drawings than photographs. For this reason, it is enlightening to compare a few hand-drawn portraits to Man Ray's photographic portraits. Examining, for example, the portrait of Erik Satie drawn by Francis Picabia and published in 1924 in *Paris-Journal*, it is clear that Picabia used Man Ray's 1922 photograph as a model — pose, composition, and everything else seem "based" on the photographic image. The same is true for portraits of Tristan Tzara and Matisse. [4]

Things were different at *Vanity Fair*. The magazine was run by Frank Crownin-shield (1872-1947), a man highly involved in the New York art scene as a member of the board of directors of the Museum of Modern Art. Crowninshield wanted *Vanity Fair* to reflect the artistic and technical developments of the day. It was thus a "society" magazine with a cultural bent, featuring music, theater, literature, painting, and photography. *Vanity Fair* was the first magazine to publish Man Ray's Paris portraits, starting in June 1922. Every issue featured artists or writers in a section headed, "We Nominate for the Hall of Fame." Thanks to portraits by Man Ray, the magazine presented, in the following order, Tristan Tzara, [5] Pablo Picasso, [6] James Joyce, [7] Gertrude Stein, [8] Augustus John, [9] Sinclair Lewis, [10] Sherwood Anderson, [11] André Derain, [12] Le Corbusier, [13] and more.

Furthermore, *Vanity Fair* devoted an entire page to various existing portraits of the marquise Casati, in which Man Ray's famous "blurred" photograph featured prominently alongside an oil portrait by Augustus John and a sculpted head by Jacob Epstein. [14] Photography was thus raised to the same level as other art forms, with a caption describing the "striking" portrait in which Man Ray revealed Casati's "gift of double vision." Study of the various painted portraits of the marquise, moreover, suggests that Man Ray's version of events (according to which his picture was the felicitous result of a technical error) is unlikely. Indeed, most portraits of the day reveal Casati's dark gaze, her heavily made-up eyes often marked by bags (see Romaine Brook's *La Marquise Casati*). It would seem more plausible to think that Man Ray, wanting to present the best possible image of his sitter, devised this way of simultaneously flattering the marquise and embodying her "gift of double vision."

Frédéric Mégret, 1929

Edward James, 1937

Edward James, 1937

For Aragon's *Aurélien*, circa 1930

Vogue, meanwhile, only began publishing Man Ray's portraits in 1924. It should also be pointed out that this magazine was more devoted to Parisian high society life than to the arts. Here Man Ray mainly published portraits of marchionesses, countesses, duchesses and other "ladies" of the day. These portraits were mostly produced in what today appears to be a "classic," not to say pictorialist, manner — the female silhouette is generally set against a golden or shimmering background, the face bathed in soft light. Man Ray nevertheless worked to give his sitters a natural pose or posture, and it is precisely this "unaffected elegance" that made him so popular.

By the year 1925, Man Ray was able to charge 1,000 francs per sitting. Only a few eccentrics allowed him to follow his own inspiration when photographing them, as was the case with the marquise Casati, mentioned above, and Lady Abdy, "one of the foreign high society beauties residing in France" who was also a rather exuberant woman according to what was said here and there. Such a sitter tolerated a certain originality while Man Ray was shooting — she posed frontally, elbows on a table, face held in her hands. She even allowed the publication of this photograph in the pages of *Vogue*, an unusual gesture for that time. [15]

As we have observed, Man Ray's approach was adapted to the client. Theater personalities (Léna Amsel, Paulette Pac, and Marcel Herrand) and dancers were shown in costume, as exemplified by Vicente Escudero, a Spanish dancer photographed at the Rue Campagne-Première studio in 1928. Dressed in his stage costume, he seems to be "dancing" for Man Ray as opposed to simply posing for the photographer. Man Ray managed to reproduce the effect of movement through shadows cast by several lamps, creating sophisticated lighting designed to satisfy publications announcing the famous dancer's performance at the Pleyel concert hall. Movement thus assumes all its scope here not because it is decomposed, but rather because, lit by several lamps, Escudero's pose endlessly echoes across the walls, creating the impression of movement.

"Bread-and-butter" portraits

Two categories of portraits must be distinguished within Man Ray's work: those he did with interest, sensitivity, attention, and creativity, and those he produced mechanically. The distinction came naturally to Man Ray. Tourists — people who wanted "family portraits" or who, more generally, did not interest Man Ray — received a portrait that met their expectations: a good, technically competent likeness. The results were "fitting," but Man Ray invested little talent in them. Most of the unidentified portraits in the MNAM archives are of this type, totaling a third of the collection (1,651 unidentified portraits out of 5,004 contact prints preserved).

In contrast, other portraits betray all the artist's sensibility. Man Ray's sharp mind and eye created a veritable pantheon of men and women who left their mark on the times. Yet many of his fine portraits are of quite ordinary people. In both instances, however, Man Ray took a liking to a face, a character, or an achievement. Daniel Masclet has said that portraitists must have "an understanding and a love of faces." [16] Man Ray had that love of faces right from youth, but he had chosen to be an artist, and people whom he felt did not recognize him as such became

15) *Vogue, vol. 6, no. 8, August 1, 1925, p. 26.*

16) *Daniel Masclet,* Réflexions sur le Portrait en Photographie, *Paris : Publications Photo-Revue, 1971, p. 15.*

17) See previous chapter, "'Authentic' Photography," p. 71.

18) Roland Barthes, La Chambre Claire : Note sur la Photographie, Paris : Cahiers du Cinéma, Gallimard, Le Seuil, 1980, p. 18.

19) "Man Ray l'enchanteur—Interview de Daniel Masclet," Photo-France, no. 10, November 1951, p. 32.

20) "Man Ray l'enchanteur...," p. 26.

21) Letter preserved in the Man Ray archives, Musée National d'Art Moderne, Paris.

22) Pierre Mac Orlan (born Pierre Dumarchey, 1882–1970) was part of the group around Guillaume Apollinaire and Max Jacob. He wrote works in which reality merges with imagination (Quai des brumes, 1927) and was also greatly interested in photography of the day, having written a book on Germaine Krull (Paris : Gallimard, 1931). His letter is preserved in the Man Ray archives at the Musée National d'Art Moderne.

Jacqueline Goddard, 1932

"objects" to photograph, clients without interest for whom it was not worth mobilizing his talent. As has been said earlier, it appears that Man Ray occasionally allowed his assistant to take the photograph. [17]

It has generally been noted that, when viewing a portrait photograph, it is the sitter one sees. The photograph itself, as Roland Barthes pointed out, remains "invisible." [18] That is why a portrait of an anonymous sitter is necessarily less interesting than one of Picasso. Man Ray adopted a somewhat different attitude. "Often enough, my finest portraits were done with ordinary people — after all, Renoir and even Rembrandt himself had their maids pose for them. They did queens with maids, and sometimes maids with queens." [19] The MNAM archives contain a great many portraits of people who, even if they have been identified, are of little interest today. The collection is therefore partly a victim of history, which dictates that the memory of some people be cultivated, that of others forgotten. Yet in most cases, notably when research has turned up traces of these people, a minimum of information about the person reveals that Man Ray literally *revealed* his sitter. One of the finest — if least known — examples of his revelatory sensitivity is Man Ray's portrait of the Pitoëffs. One need merely compare his portraits of this theatrical couple with other portraits of them to realize (assuming one "knows" them) the extent to which Man Ray was able to capture their very essence, what Barthes called "a delicate mental texture, rather than mimicry," of which only "very great portraitists" are capable. [20]

Man Ray often received complimentary letters thanking him for the portraits he did. Sitters compared his portraits to paintings. In this respect, it is worth reproducing a letter written by the poet Max Jacob on September 21, 1922, just after he converted to Catholicism and withdrew to the abbey of Saint-Benoît-sur-Loire :

My dear Man Ray,

It's a painting! What colors! Or rather, what fine values! What external brilliance! What atmosphere! Not to mention that portraits by painters are never good likenesses whereas here I'm alive, myself! Not very handsome! Not too ugly! Not made younger. No longer very young! With a large concrete nose and the fairly devilish mouth of a woman.

I'm delighted with you and with the portrait. I've written to Cocteau that I know you. That I have a portrait by you and that everyone admires it and that he would be wise to ask you for it because I cannot bring myself to part with this authentic effigy.

Thanks a million, regal Buddha.

Warmly,

Max Jacob

PS : I'll come to Paris in a month to thank you and to advertise for you, if you like. [21]

Several years later, in July 1927, it was Pierre Mac Orlan who congratulated Man Ray for a portrait "more sensitive than countless paintings." [22]

Thus little by little, everyone who counted on the Parisian artistic and literary scene visited Man Ray's studio, from actors (Marcel Herrand, Catherine Hessling) to musicians and dancers (Serge Lifar), orchestra conductors (Ernest Ansermet),

Tristan Tzara, 1924

Study for the portrait of Tristan Tzara, 1921

Tristan Tzara, 1921

André Breton, circa 1930

composers (*Le Groupe des Six*), singers (Jeanne Bathori), poets, writers, painters, and sculptors (Jo Davidson), not forgetting collectors (Edward James, Gertrude Stein), gallery owners (Jeanne Bucher), publishers (Albert Skira), the night-club crowd (Louis Moysès, who ran *Le Boeuf sur le Toit*), and fashion designers (Jean-Charles Worth, Elsa Schiaparelli, Nicole Groult). All of avant-garde Paris came "to have a portrait made."

As Sylvia Beach said, "to be 'done' by Man Ray ... meant you were rated as somebody." [23] Even in London, tourists planning to pass through Paris were advised to make a date with the photographer. In June 1935, on acquiring a studio on Rue Val-de-Grace, Man Ray even advertised it in *Minotaure*. [24]

Despite this success, Man Ray adopted a provocative attitude toward his portrait work at the time. In 1929, Jean Gallotti devoted a column titled "Is Photography an Art?" to Man Ray. "There is an entire series [of photographs] that [Man Ray] discusses only condescendingly, which turn out to be portraits recalling the English Romantic school, or else modern women with shorn heads, or actresses in theatrical poses, all handled with broad modeling and fine tones. They are, in fact, admirable. All were shot on very small negatives, and later enlarged, a method that eliminates pointless details from the final print and produces a soft yet not affected feel. For Monsieur Man Ray, however, all this is nothing but fodder for the uncouth." [25]

The chief reason for Man Ray's derogatory attitude toward his own work can be explained by the fact that portraiture was then considered to be a minor art (regardless of the medium employed). The pursuit of a likeness — theoretically inherent to portraiture — had diminished the status of artists once photography was invented, for copying was no longer considered art. With the spread of photography studios in the nineteenth century and mass access to portraiture, even painters came to devalue the portrait genre. It is worth recalling Man Ray's comment that his "painting had evolved to a degree where [he] would never consider painting a portrait." [26]

It was also the case that ever since the invention of photography, photographers — especially portraitists — were usually looked upon as failed painters. The general consensus was that only bad painters became photographers, those who could not handle a brush well enough and therefore had to employ mechanical means to reproduce reality. Man Ray must have thought long and hard before adopting this career.

Given this context, Man Ray's talent lay in his use of techniques that marked both his period and photography itself, to the extent of giving portraiture back its letters of nobility, a development sparked by his use of superimposition and above all solarization.

Only rarely did Man Ray use superimposition in portraiture. The oldest and best known example is certainly the portrait of Tristan Tzara (1921), showing the dada poet sitting atop a ladder while the nude torso of a standing woman is superimposed on the image as though printed or painted on the nearby wall. The negative of Tzara is lost, and only a negative of the bare-breasted woman is preserved in the MNAM archives, demonstrating that Man Ray produced this superimposition by printing the two negatives simultaneously [27] (or one after the other) rather than exposing the same plate several times. [28]

23) *Sylvia Beach*, Shakespeare and Company, New York : Harcourt, Brace & Co., 1959, p. 112.

24) *Man Ray had rented an apartment on Rue Val-de-Grace since 1929, but did not use it as a photo studio; the advertisement indicates that Man Ray no longer occupied Rue Campagne-Première but had not yet moved to Rue Denfert-Rochereau.*

25) *Jean Gallotti, "La photographie est-elle un art?" L'Art vivant, no. 103, April 1, 1929, p. 282.*

26) *Man Ray*, Self Portrait (1963), p. 87.

27) *A certain number of negatives in the MNAM archives are literally taped together.*

28) *The MNAM archives contain items demonstrating that Man Ray also created superimposition effects by exposing a plate several times, as seen in a previously unknown version of L'Aurore des Objets ("Dawn of Objects") combined with a seascape, and also in a fashion photograph which underscores the fluidity of a garment by combining two poses on the same negative.*

André Breton, circa 1930

29) *Rémy Duval, "Surimpression," Photo-Ciné-Graphie, no. 15, May 1935, pp. 8-9.*

30) *From a letter discovered in MNAM's Man Ray archives, dated October 12, 1934.*

31) *It should be noted, however, that Lee Miller's father was an enthusiastic amateur photographer.*

32) *"My Man Ray — An Interview with Lee Miller Penrose by Mario Amaya," Art in America, May-June 1975, p. 56.*

33) *Dominique Baqué,* Les Documents de la Modernité, *Paris : Editions Jacqueline Chambon, 1993, p. 126.*

34 *The first was published in* Arts et Métiers *in 1933, the second in* Photo-Ciné-Graphie *in 1934.*

Superimposition, like solarization, was never used solely for aesthetic ends. Rémy Duval described the effect of superimposition as follows : "Superimposition originates in the mental world. Like that mental world, it reflects the simultaneousness of ideas. It abolishes time and makes two different elements converge, like the play of memory projecting various profiles of a face onto a single surface. It merges two different dimensions, recreating the characteristics of each. It is the transposition of a musical chord into the visual sphere." [29]

Indeed, the meaning of the picture of Tzara mentioned above must not be overlooked. The superimposition shows the dada poet sitting with a hatchet and an alarm clock dangling over his head, as though time were a sword of Damocles. Yet Tzara seems unconcerned, oblivious even, and smokes a cigarette. The bare-breasted woman, far from being vulnerable, stands tall and faces front. One hand on her hip, she gazes down on the scene from her great height — the handle of the hatchet turned in her direction seems to suggest her power of decision. Since her image on the wall is transparent, she is simultaneously woman and ghost, thus representing both life and death.

Man Ray produced many solarized portraits, starting in the fall of 1929. Lee Miller claimed to have mistakenly turned on the darkroom light while negatives of Suzy Solidor were being developed. The result of such a darkroom accident had long been known under the name of the Sabattier effect, but had always been considered a defect. No one until that moment had thought of transforming it into an artistic statement. A number of studies suggest that Lee Miller and Man Ray discovered solarization together. Yet only Man Ray — an experienced, thoroughly dada artist — could have seized on chance (if indeed it was chance), error, and defect in this way. A letter addressed by Man Ray to the editor of the *New Yorker* provides a plausible explanation for the origin of his use of this darkroom effect : "I make no claims as a discoverer of outlined photographs, wrongly called 'solarizations,' which are the studied application of a phenomenon in the action of light on silver bromide, known to scientists for the past thirty years, who have tried to create emulsions to over-come it. Alfred Stieglitz is the only man I know of who fifteen years ago dared exhibit a print utilizing this violation of the photographic process." [30]

Man Ray had therefore long known of this effect. It is nevertheless possible that his "rediscovery" happened by chance, and it is probable that Lee Miller provoked the accident, since she was still a novice photographer. [31] Yet her story of being startled by a mouse in the darkroom — as recounted in an interview with Mario Amaya — is farcical. [32]

"Solarization, technically defined as a partial reversal of values in a photograph, accompanied by characteristic outlining," [33] can occur in negative or positive. Man Ray, as it happens, produced his solarizations on negatives, since the MNAM archives contain many solarized negatives and contact prints. For an artist like Man Ray, using the solarization effect on negatives allowed him to work the solarized image just like any other, on contact sheets, especially when it came to portraits, which he systematically cropped.

Although solarization presents certain technical difficulties, Man Ray always refused to disclose them. Furthermore, he was notably vexed when Maurice Tabard completely revealed the solarization process in two articles. [34]

Nusch and Sonia, 1935

Nusch and Sonia, 1935

André Breton, circa 1930

35) Man Ray, "On Photography," Commercial Art and Industry, vol. XVIII, no. 104, 1935, pp. 65-69.

36) Photo published on the cover of Time, The Weekly News Magazine, December 14, 1936

The truth is that Man Ray thought that, "as far as desires go, there is really not such a great gulf between the one who creates and the one who appreciates. Except, with the former his application may lead him too far into technical adventures, and thus create a momentary breach between himself and the spectator who, too impressed by *tours de force*, may lose sight of the original subject matter. And yet such *tours de force* when carried out without any special effort on the part of the artist, are merely means for making his subject matter more telling." [35] Technique is simply a way to express an idea. It is not a goal in itself.

In fact, Man Ray did not "solarize" everybody. On occasion, highly studied lighting during the sitting produced a portrait closer to the model's true character than solarization would have done. That was the case with Salvador Dalí, who was photographed in amazing lighting that gave his face an extravagant if not demonic effect prefiguring the legendary moustache that Dalí had not yet begun to wear. [36]

The MNAM archives contain a rich harvest of previously unknown solarized portraits, including those of Albert Skira and Tériade, confirming the popularity of the process.

It was thanks to solarization, then, that Man Ray raised photographic portraiture to the level of creative art. The technique enabled him to obtain a striking effect that astonished at the time, suggesting a materialization of a person's aura. The fact that Man Ray photographed and then solarized the most important artists of the day (Picasso, Braque, Duchamp, Breton, Max Ernst) reinforced the theory that some artists are geniuses who possess a special aura. According to the occult sciences, such auras are visible only to the initiated. Although Man Ray, unlike the other surrealists, was not a fan of seances, solarization surely played an important role in his work partly due to that phenomenon. Photography was no longer straightforward documentation, simply showing what people saw — it went further, rendering visible and materializing an individual's charisma, that invisible quality which people sense only when in the presence of someone endowed with that power. With solarization, Man Ray turned photographic portraiture into an almost magical art.

From photographing objects to "revealing" people, Man Ray therefore struggled to show everyone — from avant-garde artists to the man in the street — that photography was an artistic medium. Yet he practiced what he called the "debatable" art of portrait photography so well that he was swamped with commissions. It was precisely that success, that wealth of orders, that surfeit of portraits of people seeking notoriety — people with affectations who wanted to be photographed by Man Ray more for the signature than for the intrinsic quality of the work — that ultimately led Man Ray to adopt a somewhat cynical attitude.

Several years later, Man Ray gave vent to his disillusion. "Since I'd opened a studio where I began to practice the debatable art of photography — in order to survive, I told myself — I was invaded by all kinds of people who came to see me as though I were a doctor, in the hope that I'd heal them, through flattery, of their inferiority complex, or who came to see me because they needed photos, in the same way they went to the baker or butcher to get some bread or meat." [37]

Clearly, then, it is the "uncouth" for whom *photography is not art*.

37) Man Ray, "*Impressions très personnelles sur les années 1920–1930*," Objets de Mon Affection, *Paris : Philippe Sers, 1983, p. 40 (undated text).*

Lee Miller, 1929

Untitled, 1929

Tanya Ramm, circa 1929

Dora Maar, 1936

Dora Maar, 1936

Lee Miller, 1929

Lee Miller, circa 1930

Meret Oppenheim, 1932

Meret Oppenheim, 1932

Lee Miller, circa 1930

Retour à la raison [*Return to Reason*], 1923

Study for *Le Violon d'Ingres*, 1924

Le Violon d'Ingres, 1924

Untitled, 1927

Untitled, 1927

Kiki, 1923

Untitled [Natasha], 1931

Jacqueline, 1930

Primat de la matière sur la pensée [The Primacy of Matter over Mind], 1932

Lee Miller in Cocteau's film, *The Blood of a Poet*, 1930

Nude, circa 1930

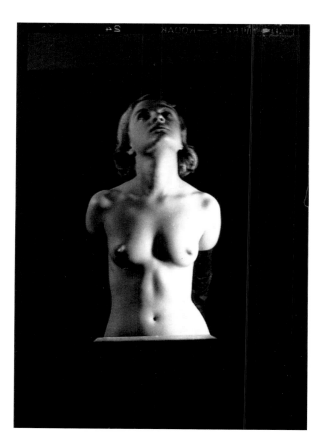

Nude female torso, circa 1930

Nude female torso, circa 1930

Kiki, circa 1925

Kiki, circa 1925

Untitled, circa 1930

Untitled, circa 1930

Lee Miller, 1930

Lee Miller, 1930

Lee Miller, 1930

Anatomies, circa 1930

Study for *Anatomies*, circa 1930

Meret Oppenheim, 1933

Meret Oppenheim, 1933

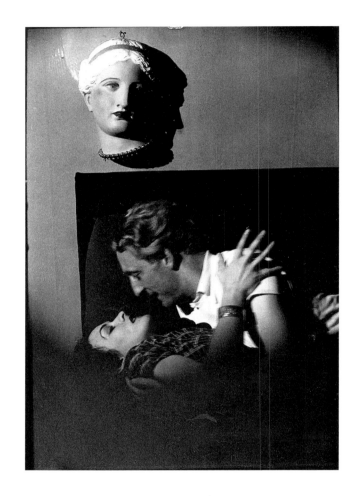

From the series *La Prière* [Prayer], circa 1930

From the series *La Prière* [Prayer], circa 1930

From the series *La Prière* [Prayer], circa 1930

From the series *La Prière* [Prayer], circa 1930

La Prière [Prayer], 1930

La Prière [Prayer], circa 1930

From the series *La Prière* [Prayer], circa 1930

Self-portrait with "dead" nude, from the series *La Prière* [Prayer], circa 1930

Érotique Voilée, 1933

Érotique Voilée, 1933

Érotique Voilée, 1933

Érotique Voilée, 1933

Érotique Voilée, 1933

Érotique Voilée, 1933

Study for *Noire et Blanche*, 1926

Le Masque [The Mask], 1926

Noire et Blanche, 1926

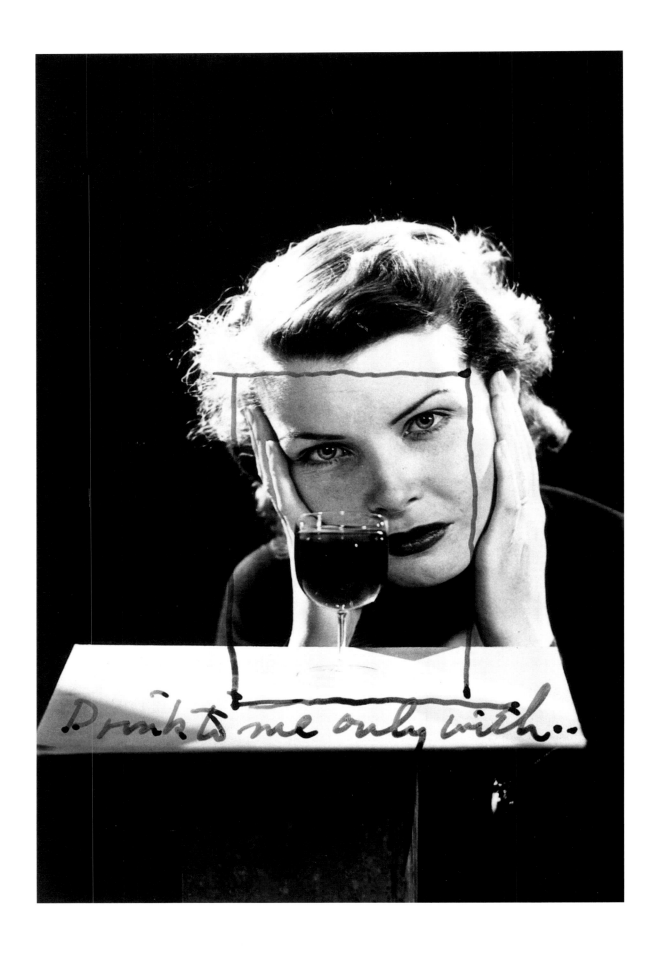

"Drink to me only with ......", circa 1932

Lydia and wooden figures, 1932

Lydia, study for *Les Larmes* [*Tears*], 1932

Les Larmes [*Tears*], 1932

Study for *L'Aurore des Objets*, 1937

Study for *L'Aurore des Objets*, 1937

L'Aurore des Objets, 1937

Study for *L'Aurore des Objets*, 1937

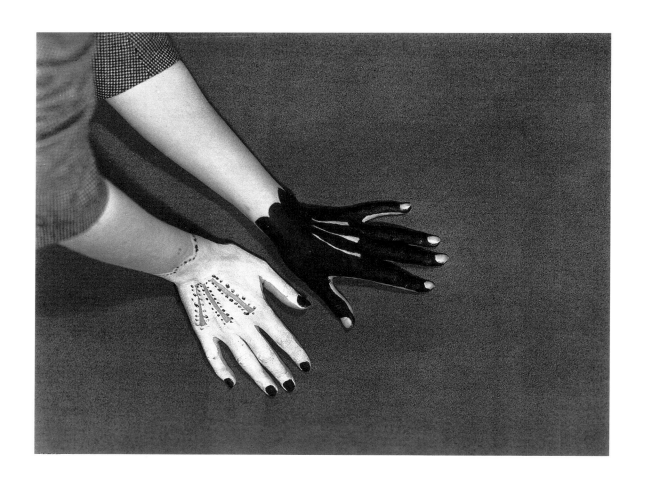

Mains Peintes par Picasso [Hands Painted by Picasso], 1935

Untitled, 1930

Untitled, 1926

Untitled, 1931

The Rayographs Floris M. Neusüss and Renate Heyne

With the rayograph Man Ray created a type of image that made all of his previous works seem like steps along a predetermined path. Even his decision in early youth to discard his family name and call himself Man Ray seems like an act of fate.

Man Ray began his career as an artist. He was exhibited at a number of New York galleries, and although he experienced a degree of success he was never quite satisfied with his painting. He varied his style, his technique, his subjects. It is possible that his encounter with Marcel Duchamp led him to analyze the reasons for this dissatisfaction. It was not a matter of the style of his painting, but of the principle of art conceived as a means to express his feelings. Ultimately, he abandoned this ambition and his painting, and turned to more technical, almost clinical methods of expression. At school his technical drawings had been considered brilliant, and his talent was greatly respected at the map and atlas publishing company where he was employed. He took up the tools he used as a draftsman — drawing pen, T-square, pencil, stencil, French curves, and airbrush — and used them to create art : pseudo-technical drawings of devices which feigned functionality and emanated precision.

Several of these works anticipate aspects that later emerge in his rayographs, e.g., a technical drawing, untitled, from 1915. This drawing features the "three-dimensional model" of the spiral and actually looks like a concept for a rayograph. The spiral reappears a little later in the "Revolving Doors" series of ten individual constructions, in which primary colored stencil-like forms are laid one on top of another to create the impression of shadows cast by different light sources. He used airbrush technique to transform positive and negative stencils into shadowlike images, finally replacing the stencils with objects that he would place directly on paper and spray. The resulting images are clear, interwoven forms surrounded by a soft hue which gives the impression of slight corporeal curves. Man Ray named these pictures "aerographs" and was extremely pleased that he was able to create them without having touched a canvas.

He taught himself photography, and since he had given up his profession as a draftsman, considered becoming a portrait photographer. After all, the camera was also a technical instrument with which one could create pictures. Man Ray collected objects made from all sorts of material and photographed them in various combinations. Following the principle Duchamp had used for his "ready-mades," he gave these works names that were totally unrelated to the subject matter. For example, in 1918 he photographed an object comprised of clothes pegs, glass, and two reflectors and gave it the name "Woman;" a photograph of an eggbeater with cast shadow he named "Man," although it is interesting to note that in 1917 he had chosen the same subject, busily spinning, for a cliché-verre and had called it simply "Eggbeater." In 1921 he decided that the titles of the images "Man" and "Woman" should be interchanged.

Man Ray had distanced himself from his subjects. He no longer tried to analyze them intellectually and portray them through his perceptions. Presentation was governed by technical means ; his only personal contribution was the title, and this he used to distance himself even further. The visual appearance of his work did

Electricité, 1931

1) *This photogram has not been found. In this context, however, a rayograph often mentioned features a black bottle, a black funnel, a black pipe stem, and a white pipe bowl on a gray background. Due to the reversal of tone values this photogram can only be the result of copying from an original. During the copying process the white pipe bowl must have been added, which strongly suggests that this particular photogram stems from a later period.*

not serve primarily as an experience for the eye, but rather as a stimulus for the spirit of the viewer.

By then the essential elements that would combine to form the rayographs were to be found in his immediate surroundings : the objects, the photography, the shadows. All that was needed to bring them together was a minor incident in the darkroom. It happened in Paris at the beginning of 1922, when sheer co-incidence brought together object, photosensitive material, and light. Man Ray instantly recognized that in the course of carrying out a routine procedure he had chanced upon a totally new genre of photograph. Working a little absentmindedly in his makeshift laboratory — his hotel room at night actually — he had unintentionally placed some objects on photographic paper and switched on the light. In simple terms that is how his first rayograph came into existence. Because the paper was already lying in developing solution he was able to observe how it turned black everywhere except where he had placed the objects. This thoroughly plausible account of the incident comes from Man Ray's book *Self Portrait*. That night he had been engaged in making prints from photographic plates (then still composed of glass) ; the photos were fashion shots featuring the clothing of Paul Poiret. At the time he did not possess an enlarger so he would place the 18 x 24 cm developed plates directly onto photographic paper to make an exposure. Through the exposure the negative image on the plate was copied onto the paper ; the paper was subsequently placed in developing solution to create a positive. At one point, without noticing, he inadvertently picked up two sheets of photographic paper together. The two sheets separated only after they had been placed in the developer, and because he did not want to throw the unexposed sheet away, he placed a glass funnel, a measuring glass and a thermometer on it and switched on the light. [1]

Droller, 1918

The photogram — in the case of Man Ray a rayograph — is therefore a photographic copying process in which flat, three-dimensional, transparent or opaque objects are placed directly onto light-sensitive paper and exposure is executed with an ordinary light bulb. It is usually a dry process and is carried out in darkroom conditions, i.e., almost total darkness. Developing takes place after exposure. Those parts of the paper which are directly exposed to light turn black, those which are covered by an object, or are unexposed, remain white. Other areas, neither covered completely nor exposed to direct light, react to refracted light which is reflected between the object and the white paper, and turn to shades of gray. The photogram, of course, is also a type of silhouette-picture, because those parts of three-dimensional objects which are not directly in contact with the paper, require only the smallest amount of light from the side in order to cast a shadow. Moholy-Nagy employed light in such a way that it governed form and the objects became unrecognizable. In contrast, Man Ray utilized light so that his objects, although slightly distorted, remain identifiable. Photograms are created principally by three effects : in places where the object is in direct contact with, or covers the light-sensitive paper, the area remains white ; the shadow of the object becomes gray ; and, the surrounding area, which is exposed directly to the light, becomes black.

With the photogram technique, Man Ray distanced himself even further from his subjects. He allowed his images to be formed by an invisible agent, light, using a method that was virtually impossible to control. The results were clear, negative forms or non-forms, as it were : although the object appears absent, a fleeting moment of contact captures its presence.

According to an account Man Ray gave in his biography *Self Portrait*,[2] it is evident that the first rayograph came into existence sometime early in 1922. He wrote : "Later that year I conceived the idea of doing an album of some prints, in a limited edition, which I called *Les Champs Délicieux*...." The *Champs Délicieux* album was published in 1922.

Frantically he set about producing rayographs which his dadaist friends received with rapturous enthusiasm. In an open letter to "Man Ray American Photographer," published in the April 1922 issue of *Les Feuilles Libres*, Jean Cocteau mentioned that Man Ray had sent him "some eighty" photograms. In the same month the Dada magazine *Le Coeur à Barbe*[3] announced that "an album of 12 original photographs would be published under the title *Les Champs Délicieux*" (the name finally became *Champs Délicieux* which made it a little less specific).

The title was chosen deliberately. It followed an example set earlier by André Breton and Philippe Soupault, who together had published a collection of "automatic texts" titled *Les Champs magnétiques*.[4] Looking back on his moment of absentmindedness, a moment in which he was carrying out a technical process routinely, Man Ray saw a psychic analogy in the discovery he had made by chance, and the principle of automatic writing.

In November 1922 the American magazine *Vanity Fair* published a one page report titled "A New Method of Realizing the Artistic Possibilities of Photography." It featured four rayographs for which Man Ray wrote the captions, and one of which alluded to his surrealistic practices : "Composition of Objects Selected With

2) Man Ray : Self Portrait, Boston 1963.

3) Le Coeur à Barbe (Tristan Tzara, editor) Issue No. 1, Paris, April, 1922.

4) André Breton, Philippe Soupault : Les Champs magnétiques, Paris 1920.

5) Laszlo Moholy-Nagy : Painting Photography Film, *Bauhaus book No. 8, Langen 1925.*

6) *André Breton :* Manifeste du Surréalisme, *in :* Poisson soluble, *Paris 1924.*

Der Sturm, n°3, 1922

Both Eyes Closed'. This suggests the modern artistic passion for machinery."

The pseudonym Man Ray turned out to be extremely fitting for an artist who became "a man who experimented with rays." The term "rayograph" derives from the pseudonym, but it also relates to the process he used to create these particular images which called for the application of light rays. Man Ray first used the term rayograph for a photogram published in the magazine *The Little Review* Number. 3, autumn issue, 1922.

Schadograph was another name given to photograms in an attempt to reflect both their character and creator. In 1919, under the influence of the Zurich Dadaists, the painter Christian Schad created the very first photograms of the 20th century. Much later, in 1936, at the exhibition "Fantastic Art, Dada, Surrealism" at the Museum of Modern Art in New York, Tristan Tzara (who had published one of Schad's photograms in 1920) christened them Schadographs : therewith blending a fundamental feature of the photogram (the shadow) with the artist's name.

The term "photogram" itself was introduced in 1925 by Laszlo Moholy-Nagy [5] and since that time it has been utilized as a generic term in many languages. Himself a reputed creator of photograms, Moholy-Nagy saw in this term an analogy with the speed of telegraphic transmission.

The very first rayographs, from which Man Ray chose 12 images for the album *Champs Délicieux*, show no identifiable signs of intentional composition. Even the light, the most important creative element of the photogram, was seldom varied. This is not a surprise if one considers that Man Ray probably wanted to follow the recommendations of André Breton in the first *Manifeste du Surréalisme*, [6] for automatic writing. Breton described it :

"Make yourself comfortable in a place where you are best able to concentrate on your inner self, then have someone bring you something to write with. Put yourself in the most passive, most receptive possible state. Forget your genius, your talent, and the talents of everyone else. Bring yourself to understand that although writing is a path that leads to all things, it is one of the most miserable to tread. Write quickly, without a preconceived theme, so quickly that you cannot remember what you have written and are not tempted to reread …."

Speed was an essential element in the production of both automatic texts and rayographs. Breton described the output of the written form thus : "The ease with which it came was self-evident. At the end of the first day we had produced around 50 pages to read to each other …."

Automatic texts produced these sorts of word streams : "I have always felt sympathy for the plants which rest on top of walls. Of all the people who slipped over me, the most beautiful, in disappearing, left me this wisp of hair, these wallflowers, without which I should have been lost to you …." which constitute in a sense a prefiguration of the rayograph. The encounter of a grater, a scoop, pencils and cotton balls is a step, a "guide to the spirit" which "little by little confirms the supreme reality of these images. Initially, the spirit contents itself simply to tolerate them, but soon it realizes that they support its intelligence and deepen its insight. The spirit becomes aware of infinity, a place where wishes are formed, where pro and contra constantly strive to outdo each other, where its confusion does not betray it. It pursues its path, inspired by these enchanting images, images

Untitled, 1922

which hardly leave it time to apply a cooling breath to its inflamed fingers. It is the most splendid of nights, the night of lightning storms ; compared to such a night, day is night." So wrote Breton in the same 1924 manifesto on the subject of automatic writing.

Marcel Duchamp enjoyed speculation over circumstances which revealed themselves "as soon as the rules of physics and chemistry were relaxed a little." [7] From Henri Poincaré's statement, "That which is not thought is absolutely nothing ....," [8] Duchamp reached the converse conclusion that if something could comprise a thought, it could also exist. In one of his mind games he proposed that since it was known that the third dimension could be presented as a projection in the second, it followed that the third dimension is actually a projection of the fourth, the fourth a projection of the fifth, and so on.

To this end he studied projections of all kinds, in theory and in practice. He invited Man Ray into his New York studio to photograph shadows of ready-mades and other objects piled up here and there, and it is likely that this exercise added impetus to Man Ray's own studies of shadow. Duchamp saw in Poincaré's writing a challenge to detach thought from hard fact. His pictures and objects were rough drafts from which logic was suspended and "truth" had no claim. Man Ray adopted this philosophy and endowed it with poetic form in his photograms. He rejected the generally safe methods of photography, which took it for granted that its images were "true." In the photogram he discovered a totally different way of seeing things, one that was ambiguous and multifaceted, one that had nothing in common with the conventional. His rayographs seem to have assumed the idea that visible reality is only a shadow projected by an exterior truth.

In autumn 1922 the forty copies of the album *Champs Délicieux* [9] were ready. Tristan Tzara wrote a foreword which he called "La Photographie à l'envers," which anticipates Man Ray's 1934 description of the proper but disrespectful way an artist deals with his materials. Man Ray would write that the "violation of the medium employed is the most perfect assurance of the author's convictions. A certain amount of contempt for the material employed to express an idea is indispensible to the purest realization of this idea." [10] Photography apparently welcomed such treatment and revealed to Man Ray its most secret and most fertile fields.

Individual photos in the album were not given titles : the photographic medium deals with the concrete in such a way that — once the actors have quit the stage — a title would destroy rather than bolster the impression of strangeness and dream. In this vein yet another parallel can be drawn with *Champs magnétiques* : in Breton's first *Manifeste du Surréalisme*, he "allowed" himself the "slight criticism" of Soupault "for giving titles to certain pages of the book — even if done with the intention of enhancing the mystification."

Almost half of Man Ray's output of rayographs was produced within two to three years of his "discovery." By the end of 1922 he had exhausted all of the formal possibilities that the photogram of objects could offer under the conditions in which he worked. Thus, for example, between exposures he might remove objects or add others ; sometimes he held objects or his own hands between the light source and the photographic paper, without letting them come into contact

7) in : Michel Sanouillet : Marcel Duchamp, Duchamp du signe, Paris 1975

8) Henri Poincaré : La Valeur de la science, Paris 1905.

9) Today there are only 20 known copies still in existence.

10) in Man Ray's text : "The Age of Light", in James Thrall Soby, editor, Photographs by Man Ray 1920 Paris 1934 (Hartford, Conn., James Thrall Soby, 1934). The text appeared first in the magazine Minotaure, 1., No. 3/4, Paris, October/December 1933.

Untitled, 1922

with the paper — this produced the effect of a soft, out of focus image, superimposed over the original object. The items he transformed in his rayographs were taken from his immediate surroundings. They were completely normal objects he used in everyday life, most of which fitted into the 18 x 24 cm format : his drawing tools, glasses, light bulbs, photographic and laboratory equipment, an egg, prisms, rolls of film, sand, souvenirs and small fetishes, pieces of jewelry, cooking utensils, cotton wool, flowers, spirals, pubic hair, hands, heads, and also — as was the case with his airbrush work — some of his 'Objects of Affection' (e.g., the "Lampshade"). He did not leave home in search of his material, but instead chose items that were intimately domestic in character.

Of some images two or three variations are known. In retrospect, however, it is clear that they did not result from attempts at systematic improvement. The twelve motifs that appeared in *Champs Délicieux* were all created by following the same method : He used a single light source which always came from the same direction, made only one exposure, and did not move or change the position of the objects because this would have robbed them of their identity. Only the second image remains mysterious, since it features positive and negative forms side by side — an impossibility given the basic photographic process he was using. The reversal of the tone values in this picture resulted neither from solarization nor from some other process of partial inversion, whatever part mirrored reflections may have played. It is important to remember that Man Ray created these images in his hotel room, an environment that was hardly conducive to technical experimentation, even if he had been so inclined.

Perhaps this negative/positive rayograph was the result of an attempt to create the motifs for the album on film (in his case on 18 x 24 cm photographic plates), rather than on the same size photographic paper, since in order to create the 40 copies of *Champs Délicieux*, he had to reproduce each image 40 times without a substantial loss of tonality. For this he used a camera with an 18 x 24 cm glass negative from which the images were copied directly onto paper. It is conceivable that during the process he attempted to create a photogram directly on a glass plate. Copying from this glass plate would of course produce a positive image — black forms on a white background — and would have been completely lacking in the characteristic which made his rayographs so fascinating : namely, a form brilliant in clarity and aura. It was an idea he abandoned rather quickly, allowing it to come to light only in this puzzling image (probably the result of copying a photogram from film and at the same time combining it with other objects, possibly a stencil).

With these photograms Many Ray accomplished a classic work of surrealism, at a time when surrealism was still in its infancy. He recognized that photograms automatically transcended the worldly form of objects by transforming them into "creatures of light." His photograms expose the extraordinary qualities of things ordinary, but each item — pipe, light bulb, funnel — remains identifiable. A contrasting program was that of Moholy-Nagy whose photograms — almost half of his entire oeuvre — were exhibited at the Centre Georges Pompidou in 1995. He allowed the form of his objects, all of which were things he found in his studio, to disappear completely. By multiplying both the sources of light and the exposures, and in moving his objects around, he rendered them unrecognizable. They do not, however, convey the impression of abstract composition. On the contrary, one senses clearly that the objects from which the forms derive were once present, and recognizes that through light they have been transformed. These images beautifully illustrate the remarkable qualities of light and its creative power.

In 1931 Man Ray produced a portfolio of ten photograph/photogram combinations which the Paris Electricity Board (CPDE) published in a limited edition of 500 copies titled *Electricité*. In creating this series he pushed the possibilities of the photogram even further, concentrating on their ability, through light and transparency, to elevate "things" to the level of idol. The resultant images appear to be charged with a universal energy, like stars in a dark universe.

In the foreword to *Electricité*, Pierre Bost contemplated that electricity as a phenomenon is "no more comprehensible to us than a sunrise, a shooting star, a rainbow or a flash of lightning would have been to prehistoric man." Man Ray, in his portrayal of the phenomenon, presents it as a willing servant, albeit one endowed with the fascination of the inexplicable. This servant will undertake any task with which he is confronted, no matter how large or how small; for example, he is capable of lighting the entire city of Paris, or, admitted to the intimate sphere of the bathroom, will generate warmth and comfort. The photogram effectively communicates the extremely close contact man has with electrical devices, but at the same time renders them invisible, as is the mysterious energy that drives them. Man Ray placed electricity on the same level as the familiar power of eroticism — it functions yet we do not understand how. Through the combination of photography and photogram, the picture — the intimate connection to the inconceivable device — bridges the gap between the idol and its sphere of action.

In the series of ten images published in *Electricité*, Man Ray begins with a portrayal of cosmic energy (also titled "Electricité"); in the second, "Le Monde," he shows us a darkened Earth, a world that wants to be lit at night — and light, of course, he makes readily available: one simply has to reach out for the switch. On the next leg of the journey he arrives in the sparkling city of Paris, "La Ville," by night, and enters "La Maison;" in the "Salle de bains" he observes the lady of the house operating curious devices, watching closely as she irons her "Lingerie;" later he drops into "La Cuisine" and "La Salle à manger;" finally "Le Souffle" fans him a little air so that at last in the closing picture (also titled "Electricité") he can yield to the electric thrill of eroticism.

With these titles Man Ray places us at varying distances from each image: "Le Monde" presents the light side of the moon seen from the earth by night, and the switch holds the promise that, if turned on, it could be just as light here as it is there. In the "Cuisine" we see the potential consequences of using energy to excess in a roast chicken that appears to be slightly burnt. The title "La Maison" he has given to the photogram of a lampshade: it reminds us of the light it is capable of reflecting (thanks to the Paris Electricity Board), and acts as an ironic symbol for the soft, warm comforts of home. In the final image the cosmic energy of the first picture transforms itself into erotic electricity, and it is at this point at the very latest, that the observer feels the stimulus of cerebral (electric) impulses and a release of spiritual energy.

Untitled, 1923

In the 1940s Man Ray decided to give the name "Objects of my Affection" to miscellaneous objects which he had transformed by adding or eliminating some of their parts, together with furniture he made for his own use. In creating a portrait of each object, he subjected it to sympathetic photographic treatment. Clearly his power to imagine the inanimate as animate was so strong that he actually developed true affection for these "things." Man Ray's erotic treatment of certain objects created another avenue of access to his rayographs. If, with a little humor, the eggbeater of 1918 reduced eroticism to basic mechanics, then the rayographs — authentic portrayals of encounters, contact, penetration, superimposition and delicate movements — excited a spiritual form of voyeurism unknown until then. In this type of voyeurism intuitive recognition of the erotic is sublimated by a double irritation : that which is presented is not in itself erotic (only the method of presentation suggests the personal). One does not actually see what is being presented because, to some extent, it is only visible through its absence.

In some rayographs of the *Champs Délicieux* period he abandoned the automatic process in favor of a more deliberate method involving several steps. In the rayograph of 1923 titled "Colifichet" for example, he made a stencil by tearing a rhombus-like shape from the center. For the first exposure he placed the stencil on photographic paper, and placed within the hole a small, upright tube and a dressmaker's pin. After the first exposure, he placed the rhombus-like shape he had removed from the original stencil over the empty space, but slightly lower. During the process one of the upper corners of the rhombus curled up and threw a shadow. He removed the stencil and replaced it with the cake doily and the candle. Then he made the second exposure. (It is also possible that these two steps were undertaken in the reverse order.)

In 1934 a series of 20 rayographs were published in his book titled *Photographs by Man Ray 1920 Paris 1934*. One of these, a theatrical scene, features similar imagery : a rhombus-like form fades upwards in the slot of an opening stage curtain to reveal a delicate cloud of pubic hair. Next to it, waiting, is a square glass rod.

Each chapter of this book contains a brief preface, the texts by Man Ray himself, Paul Eluard, André Breton, Marcel Duchamp, and Tristan Tzara (who had already sung the praises of rayographs in *Champs Délicieux*). The first chapter is devoted to photographs of objects (for example, his home-made furniture), various structures, stones and plants ; the second shows female nudes, and the third "The Visages of Women ;" following the chapter featuring portraits of famous men, the rayographs — the pictures of absent objects — bring the book to a close. Introduced by Tzara's text , "When things dream," the photograms begin with three automatic images from the *Champs Délicieux* period, become progressively more erratic but equally more refined, and conclude with one generally referred to as "Man Ray Kissing Kiki."

His own introduction to the book Man Ray titled "The Age of Light," which was a direct reference to his rayographs. He wrote : "It is in the spirit of an experience and not of experiment that the following autobiographical images are presented. Seized in moments of visual detachment during periods of emotional contact, these images are oxidised residues, fixed by light and chemical elements, of living organisms." [11]

11) in Man Ray's text :"The Age of Light", in James Thrall Soby, editor, Photographs by Man Ray 1920 Paris 1934 (Hartford, Conn., James Thrall Soby, 1934). The text appeared first in the magazine Minotaure, 1., No. 3/4, Paris, October/December 1933.

Untitled, 1927

Untitled, 1943

Untitled, 1925

Colifichet [Frippery], 1923

Untitled, 1924

Untitled, 1945

Untitled, 1923

Untitled, 1945

Untitled, 1923

Untitled, 1923

Untitled, 1922

Head, New York, 1920

DENATURING REALITY

Photography as a Depiction of Non-Euclidean Space

In addition to good, routine photography, or the more elaborate work marked by the use of clearly "artistic" effects (solarization, double exposures, rayographs, etc.), Man Ray explored a still narrower path where discoveries were more unpredictable yet more promising.

The camera thereby became a way to shatter the fundamental ambiguity of the world. As early as 1918, Man Ray used it not only to challenge standard conventions of perspective (as modernist photographers would do when they adopted new "angles"), but also to underscore the indeterminate nature of photographed reality. Without wanting to assert a direct correlation between the publication of new scientific theories and the new visual idiom explored by Man Ray, his efforts now appear striking in the way they placed photography at the center of one of the major aesthetic debates of the day.

Integration of Shadows, 1919

L'Homme, 1920

La Femme, 1920

Coat Stand, 1920

Duchamp and Man Ray : Exchanging Glances

Michel Sanouillet

Recent decades have seen a proliferation of studies both of Man Ray and Marcel Duchamp. Light has been shed on practically every aspect of their respective achievements, from different angles and from different parts of the globe. Shadowy areas remain, of course, along with unknown or unused material. In general, however, it can be said that the lives and works of the two men are now as familiar as those of their well-known contemporaries.

More pertinent to this exhibition, the relationship of both artists to photography has been the subject of lengthy and often relevant study, [1] not to mention the exhaustive exhibition catalogues. Man Ray's enormous contribution to modern art was little known, underestimated or misunderstood until recently, yet has now been quantitatively and artistically reassessed in its diversity. Today we realize that he was not only the "twentieth-century Nadar" but that as a painter, filmmaker, and creator of objects as well as photographer, he was able, beginning in his early New York period, to play on all possible combinations ; he successively (or simultaneously) employed canvases, pigments, lenses, and "things," assigning them all roles beyond the scope of ordinary usage and effectively scrambling the picture.

Correspondences

It is nevertheless worth dwelling for a moment on the relationship between Man Ray and his friend Marcel Duchamp, attempting to detect points of convergence and divergence, explaining the special status conferred on them by the contemporary art world in both America and Europe.

Comparison of the symmetrical careers of the two artists may well astonish future generations. One was the son of Brooklyn immigrants, the other a young, provincial Frenchmen from an affluent family in Normandy, who would normally have become a local notable like his father — what mischievous sprite could have brokered their encounter and subsequent journey down parallel paths ?

Everything, at the outset, should have kept them apart — geography, language, culture, education, history, social status, political tendencies. And yet two lines from Baudelaire come stubbornly to mind whenever I recall their silhouettes :

> *Comme de longs échos qui de loin se répondent*
> *En une ténébreuse et profonde unité ....*
>
> [Like long echoes answering one another from afar
> in deep and somber unison]

Having visited them often in the two decades prior to their deaths, I was frequently able to sense the physical and spiritual brotherhood linking the two men.

As individuals, first : they were approximately the same age (Duchamp was born in 1887, Man Ray in 1890) and, like Picabia, belonged to the older generation of dadaists (Breton, Aragon, Tzara, and Eluard were ten years younger). This spurred a certain complicity born of joint action. Striking similarities also marked their instinctive reactions, their gestures, behavior, attitudes, tastes and

1) Jean Clair, Duchamp et la Photographie, Paris : Le Chêne, 1977.

Marcel Duchamp, Bonds for Monte-Carlo roulette, 1924

preferences, their relationships, friendships, character traits, lifestyles. Their general attitude toward existence has been rendered more understandable by Paul Feyerabend's text on the "lightness of dadaist being." [2]

With his inimitable humor, Man Ray recounted his first meeting with Duchamp, who came to visit him in the company of Walter Arensberg in 1915 at the little house in Ridgefield, New Jersey, that he shared with "Donna" (Adon Lacroix). [3] Despite their ignorance of each other's language, they immediately found themselves on the same wavelength. Over the years, a few pithy phrases marked their entente. Duchamp used to say, "Yes, we're very fond of each other — we play chess and we don't have children." To Duchamp's famous statement that "There's no solution, because there's no problem," Man Ray replied, "I have no problems, I only have solutions."

Both of them tried to take their complementary and contradictory experiments to the limit: painting without a brush (air-brushing), then without canvas, then without use of the human hand, letting machines drive the artwork, abandoning plan or goal, taking chances, always going further just to see, to see ....

Even without referring to texts or images, it is easy to see that, as their respective oeuvres evolved, innovations came to light almost simultaneously, according to a mode of remote communication that recalls DNA's double helix. It is possible to cite dozens of works that emerged at the same moment from their respective studios, yet accompanied by a silent inflection that saved them from absolute similarity. All along their parallel paths, from the Ridgefield meeting onward, a "mirroring effect" can be observed in their output: one echoed the other, harmonically rather than fundamentally identical. The effect was sometimes the fruit of deliberate collaboration, usually a distant exchange between two symbiotic minds. This type of echoing creativity has been noted between certain dadaists, especially between Picabia and Duchamp during the period of mechanomorphic canvases (New York, 1915–1920), although never so obstinately nor over so long a period.

Man Ray and Duchamp shared a love of experimentation elevated into unwritten dogma — the gift of inventiveness in its natural state. Both of them clearly found it impossible not to create. This led to all those things they did together, pell-mell: optical machines and cinematic experiments, "a-paintings," indulgence in games of chance, chess and chessboards, the New York dada publications, the founding of the Société Anonyme, fascination with magical objects and inventions. The close relationship between Duchamp's "ready-mades" and Man Ray's "objects of my affection" leaps to the eye. No difference of execution or intention can be perceived between the latter's *Gift* and the former's *Trébuchet*. Puns, mockery, sophisticated enigmas: *L'Enigme d'Isidore Ducasse* [*The Riddle*] is echoed by *Ready-Made à Bruit Secret* [Ready-Made with Secret Sound]. To hark back to Baudelaire once again, forms, ideas, and sounds echo one another.

One might establish, for example, an interesting parallel between research into the photographic handling of the image, notably Man Ray's solarizations, and certain works by Duchamp such as the *Portrait du Dr. Dumouchel* (April 1910) where the doctor's body is bathed in a halo or "miraculous aura" (Duchamp *scripsit*). Forty years later, the Soviet engineer Semen Kirlian would discover the aural doubling or "Kirlian effect," an electroluminescent phenomenon specific to living structures, characterized by a coronal image around the photographic plate of the subject.

2) Paul Feyerabend, Contre la Méthode, Paris : Le Seuil, 1979.

3) Man Ray, Self Portrait, Boston : Little, Brown, 1988, p. 56.

Divergences

And yet, the oneness of tone and meaning in the works and lives of the two friends cannot mask the differences that guarantee the originality of each man. Study of these disparities should not be limited, however, to a superficial list of points of dissimilarity. An heuristic tool is required to develop a global and exhaustive explanation of the feeling that Marcel Duchamp and Man Ray were each stamped with a fundamental originality that brooked neither copy nor replica.

The most convenient, if not the newest, tool is supplied by the typology elaborated by Pierre Bourdieu in his writings on the sociology of art. In his best known volume, *La Distinction, Critique Sociale du Jugement*, he showed how social background influences individual and collective behavior toward the products of artistic activity. [4] On one hand there is what he calls "legitimate" art, produced by and aimed at the "bourgeois" classes, developed and disseminated through traditional channels of cultural transmission, namely family school, college, church, army, and all establishment organizations whose goal is to elaborate and perpetuate tradition, that is to say develop a tree of cultural heritage for the dominant classes.

Each class has its own cultural domain. At the top are those who, although ignorant of much specialized knowledge, are able to locate it on a given branch of the tree of acquired information and therefore give the impression of having genetically received, so to speak, culture without having made an effort to acquire it. This is the realm of bourgeois aestheticism and eclecticism.

In counterpoint, "working-class aesthetics" is a *dominated* aesthetic which must constantly define itself in relation to dominant aestheticisms. [5] Each of the dominated classes is called upon to imitate, to the extent of its possibilities, artistic fields circumscribed by the upper class, considered to be the sole heir to artistic legitimacy. Having neither the financial resources nor the essential cultural institutions, a dominated class invents impoverished substitutes inspired by the legitimate cultural property it covets : thus operetta emerges in counterpoint to opera, movies to theater, records to concerts, collections of key-rings to collections of pre-Columbian statuettes.

Two methods of acquiring culture are therefore presented :

"Total, precocious, and painless learning, practiced from early childhood within the family, extended by academic learning which presupposes and completes it, as distinguished from later, methodical, accelerated learning not so much by the depth and durability of its effect — as the ideology of cultural 'polish' would have it — as by the modality of the language and culture that it furthermore tends to inculcate. It confers the self assurance that goes with the certainty of possessing the cultural legitimacy and ease identified with excellence ; it produces a paradoxical relationship, displayed by the old bourgeoisie, of confidence in (relative) ignorance and casual familiarity with culture, perceived as a kind of family property that has been legitimately inherited." [6]

Duchamp : eclectic, legitimate art

This latter picture seems to apply to Duchamp rather well. Raised in a close-knit,

4) Pierre Bourdieu, La distinction, Critique Sociale du Jugement, *Paris : Editions de Minuit, 1979, passim. The following quotations are translated directly from the French. (Cf. English translation by Richard Nice under the title of* Distinction, *Cambridge, Mass : Harvard University Press, 1984.)*

5) Bourdieu, p. 42, fn.

6) Bourdieu, p. 71.

affluent milieu, he received a classical education at the primary and secondary level, and passed his "baccalauréat" (a highly valued diploma at the time) at the Lycée Corneille in Rouen. Despite his intellectual bent, he did not shrink from technical training as a print-making "artisan," having inherited etching genes from his grandfather Emile Nicolle a well-known engraver. Strongly rooted in Normandy, and imbued with a sharp sense of family, Duchamp often returned to Rouen for reunions with his five brothers and sisters.

Thus he never had to worry about making a name (already taken, for that matter, by his two elder brothers, Raymond and Jacques) ; at the most, he would have to make his first name. He failed to get into the Ecole des Beaux-Arts in Paris, but attended, with no illusions, a private art studio called Académie Julian. Although on his own financially, he had enough elbow room to give free rein to his independent — indeed, libertarian — tendencies. He was neither ambitious nor concerned with success. His capital was composed not of money but of the symbolic property inherited from the family.

He therefore remained largely untroubled by financial problems throughout his life. He survived one way or another on minor jobs (librarian, French teacher, art adviser and broker, etc.). Later, he married Alexina Sattler, Pierre Matisse's first wife, reestablishing contact between himself and the art world.

He was a true dilettante, his life based on an innate sense of his own legitimacy, a source of security and confidence in a future guided by a strong if invisible thread. Although he went through difficult times just as everyone else did (notably during the two world wars), he did not show it.

Duchamp felt no need to tell his own story. Unlike Man Ray, he did not publish a biography or memoirs. Duchamp never indulged in that type of confession. He deliberately let silence reign over everything that concerned him personally, the events and incidents of his private or social life. It took the recollections of a few friends, plus the perseverance of Jacques Caumont, to assemble the scrupulous ephemerides that constitute the almanac of his existence. [7]

Duchamp's correspondence was often swift and superficial. He displayed sovereign haughtiness and affable serenity in the face of everyday incidents. He projected the outward appearance of a deliberately hieratic sphinx, with an enigmatic, Mona Lisa smile.

The term that might describe Duchamp's demeanor at any given moment is the sense of being *at ease*. As Bourdieu wrote, "Material or symbolic consumption of the art work constitutes a supreme sign of ease (with which excellence is identified) in the simultaneous meanings of condition and attitude that ordinary language gives to that word." [8]

Appearances were misleading. From those still waters would surge an intellectual rebellion, the most insidious of the twentieth century insofar as it sought to smash mental structures with powerful social roots.

His was a rebellion, not a revolution — and a solo rebellion at that. As Yeats pointed out, art is a social act by a lone individual. Indeed, it took a person sufficiently strong and undeniably legitimate to *validate aesthetically* ordinary or even "uncouth" objects (those aesthetically appropriated — or not — by the "uncouth," as in the ready-mades, for instance). [9]

7) See Jacques Caumont and Jennifer Gough-Cooper, Ephemerides On and About Marcel Duchamp and Rrose Sélavy, Cambridge, Mass : MIT Press, 1993.

8) Pierre Bourdieu, "Anatomie du Goût," Actes de la Recherche en Sciences Sociales, no. 5, October 1976, Paris, p. 21.

9) Bourdieu, La Distinction..., p. 41.

Joseph Stella and Marcel Duchamp

Man Ray : indiscriminate, illegitimate art

The other part of Bourdieu's picture would seem to cover Man Ray's particular case. Born into a poor Jewish immigrant family of Russian extraction, he spent his childhood in the "difficult" borough of Brooklyn, New York. He did well at elementary school and high school, was highly gifted in mechanical drawing, considered and then rejected a career as architect. He was curious about everything, and gifted in everything, yet seemed to have difficulty finding a direction in life. He frequented the anarchistic Francisco Ferrer art center as well as, from 1905 onward, Alfred Stieglitz's Photo-Secession Gallery, known as 291. He thereby closely linked painting and photography with an atmosphere of libertarian effervescence. He acquired the rudiments of literary culture through his first wife, the Belgian-born poet Adon Lacroix.

The social milieu in which Man Ray took root fully corresponds to Bourdieu's "illegitimate" category. Born on American soil, he was brought up on that country's founding values : Weber's redeeming ethic of work and money, the capitalist myth of the self-made man who starts with nothing but who owes everything to hard work and determination. Under these conditions, as a man of acquired culture, he could not entertain the casual relationship with culture that permitted the freedom and boldness displayed by those who possessed it by birthright, that is to say by nature and essence.

Throughout his *Self Portrait*, Man Ray recounts the ins and outs of his everyday adventures in an anecdotal style. As delightful and appealing as it is, this picaresque novel — highly lucid, disarmingly frank, alternately warm and vindictive — paints the uncompromising picture of a man caught in the storm of events, grumbling (sometimes brooding) about men (and women). His attractive character seems much more human, moving, freer and easier to grasp than Duchamp's. Although mystery remains, neither the life nor works of Man Ray are shrouded in darkness.

It was only in the occasional foreword to exhibition catalogues that Man Ray indulged in considerations of a more general order, suggesting that he had indeed thought deeply about major human issues. He followed an uncertain path governed by life's vicissitudes, chance encounters, and a feeling of financial insecurity. He was often anxious, uncomfortable, and linguistically tongue-tied in good (and critical) French circles, despite having many friends and "rubbing elbows" with high society.

Photography as a middling — but not minor — art

Frequently penniless, unsure of the future, not having Duchamp's naturally carefree attitude, Man Ray felt a need for recognition and social status. Simultaneously he feared being stuck in the role of art photographer (like Karsh or Harcourt) or darkroom wizard, as this would undermine his status as painter, or legitimate artist.

Indeed, the legitimate castes of the 1930s still considered photographic technique to be a derivative art. Because it was more accessible than painting, it was reserved for people "devoted to motley fields and middle arts, among which were recruited most of the fervent photographers, jazz and film specialists, or operetta lovers."[10]

10) Bourdieu, "Anatomie du Goût," p. 37. See also Pierre Bourdieu et al., Un Art Moyen, les Usages Socieaux de la Photographie, Paris : Editions de Minuit, 1965, passim.

As an intrinsically utilitarian medium, photography was granted aesthetic validity only for the information it conveyed and for the legibility of that information, which led to Man Ray's feeling of awkwardness during the period of his society portraits.

What truly interested Man Ray were precisely the impoverished substitutes for "chic" objects and practices — objects yanked out of context, incongruous and provocative paintings, photographs whose meaning was found only in the images themselves. Yet his public was probably disoriented by the variety of subjects and techniques he employed, making it hard to judge or distinguish between what was legitimate and what was crudely indiscriminate. As Man Ray himself pointed out, he was disturbed by the idea of having to stick with fixed, recognizable style, for it would turn painting into a colossal bore. He was an artist seeking an identity, without managing to find one.

Convergences

According to Bourdieu's typology, Man Ray and Duchamp were predestined to "go with the grain" of their social categories, Duchamp in the cosy realm of the cream of bourgeois society, Man Ray within the disjointed culture of America's *uomo qualunque* ("man in the street"). Yet it so happened that both found themselves, at the end of a long and chaotic road, liberated or excluded from their respective classes. They reconciled illegitimacy with eclecticism, legitimacy with disorder. This was something not anticipated by Bourdieu, himself a prisoner of Marxian analysis in which social environment inescapably and inexorably seals the fate of individuals and societies.

The fact is that the indiscriminate has become legitimate in today's artistic context. Industrial objects, diverted from their original purpose, now hold pride of place alongside Rembrandts in the most famous collections. If Duchamp's original urinal were to turn up, the most glamorous galleries in the world would shamelessly offer extravagant bids at Christie's. During the 1988 Man Ray exhibition in Washington, monumental reproductions of his *Object to Be Destroyed* (metronome) swept their inquisitorial, mocking eyes over the steps of official buildings in the U.S. capital, even as the nation's Smithsonian Institute elevated little Emmanuel Radnitsky to the rank of "An American Master."

The approach followed by both men, totally spontaneous and unconscious at first, slowly took the form of a unified set of theoretical concepts over the years, which appears to us today to represent a new socio-artistic model. It is safe to say that it will survive over and above national and linguistic cultures, racial and geographic borders, and that as the century draws to a close it will thrive thanks to numerous imitators — indeed forgers — as well as authentic heirs.

We are witnessing the rehabilitation of the indiscriminate at the expense of eclecticism and salonesque aestheticism. Dada in general — and Man Ray and Duchamp in particular — overturned the establishment's tendency to impose order. They granted titles of nobility, so to speak, to middling art forms once consigned to daily consumption by the proletarian classes. For Man Ray, this meant abandoning the constraining Graflex of his early days for rayographs, and later for the rediscovery of chromatic emulsions that had so delighted nineteenth-century pictorialists.

Transatlantic, 1921

Duchamp's personal path, modus operandi, and implementation were identical. They ultimately convey extreme coherence when considered with enough distance and height so that every calculated gesture, every thought, every idea, every work (thing done), every word and text (things said) takes its place, like so many dots in a pointillist painting that requires a certain density of points before it suddenly congeals meaningfully.

The intention to invert or transgress limits, as constantly manifested by Duchamp's oeuvre, ultimately obliges the legitimate intelligentsia to recognize this very transgression of limits as an *aesthetic*.

The concomitance of the two men's approaches was patent even prior to their encounter, and it could be said that intellectually they were fated to meet despite an unfavorable historical and geographic conjuncture. They shared the same purpose, same process, same result — abolishing the distinction made by Bourdieu (who, moreover, remains superbly ignorant of dada, Duchamp, and Man Ray). One of them — Duchamp — started from a covert conceptualization of how to execute a fundamental challenge to bourgeois aestheticism, while the other — Man Ray — began empirically, from the outside, by turning products of lower-class aesthetics against that aesthetic, until everything resulted in a new, original cultural product accessible to all, transcending both proletarian color prints and aristocratic old masters.

One might legitimately wonder why it took so long for the general public to appreciate the true value of work of Man Ray and Marcel Duchamp. I remember having questioned Duchamp on this point. He told me that it was only natural, since no art dealer could have backed and defended someone like himself, who had produced so few saleable objects, or like Man Ray who created so many diverse pieces with no apparent link between them. "We were both stricken with a crippling vice — we couldn't repeat ourselves."

A reading of the books now available, covering the quasi-totality of the works of Man Ray and Marcel Duchamp, indeed gives this impression of an inextricable jumble. Nothing fulfills our insatiable appetite for order and logic. Yet beneath this apparently heterogeneous clutter lies the hint of a source of endless, unknown riches.

Collection d'Hiver [Winter Collection], 1936

Enough Rope, 1944

Le Bouquet, 1935

Feu d'Artifice [Fireworks], 1934

Lee Miller, circa 1930

Silhouette, 1930

Anatomies, 1929

Untitled, 1933

Minotaure, 1933

Explosante-fixe, 1934

Prou del Pilar, study for *Explosante-fixe*, 1934

Prou del Pilar, study for *Explosante-fixe*, 1934

Beyond Mirroring the Object   Alain Sayag

What is so original about Man Ray's oeuvre? What makes it unique among the particularly worthy output of photographers in Paris between 1922 and 1936?

Perhaps the source of his originality lay, as suggested by Herbert Moderings and Michel Sanouillet, in his enduring relationship with Marcel Duchamp and in his poorly understood determination to show us another way of grasping the sensible world. Man Ray, who was no theorist, allegedly used the means at his disposal — most notably photography — to attempt to convey this new experience.

Although he practiced the trade of photographer on a daily basis, providing magazines and other clients with competent "hackwork",[1] he strove to distinguish it from what he called his "creative productions," which he felt demanded "the same deference accorded to a work of art."[2] He noted that certain ideas "demanded a more flexible medium for their expression than the rigidity of the camera," which he had taken "to the limits of [his] inventive capacities," and that only painting enabled him to avoid "daily routine".[3] Yet he immediately added that if he had had access to the technical means to make a huge enlargement of Lee Miller's lips, which he placed in the sky above the landscape of *A l'Heure de l'Observatoire — Les Amoureux [Observatory Time — The Lovers]*, he would have willingly abandoned the boring, repetitive manual chore that occupied him almost every morning for nearly two years, in favor of another, more efficient and less painstaking method, such as photography. And although he added that he painted only what he could not photograph — things that sprang from the imagination, dreams, or a "subconscious impulse,"[4] he did not intend to establish an opposition between what he painted and what he photographed.

It would therefore be misleading, within Man Ray's work, to set photography and painting against one another. As René Crevel pointed out, "photography is not painting..., yet [Man Ray's] photography is not photography, that is to say not just a copy. He knows how to raise the key issues — the ones that arise from the spectacle of the world. So when it comes to a corkscrew, the legs of the Eiffel Tower, or a piece of sugar, [he] forces us to ask whether the corkscrews, Eiffel Tower legs and pieces of sugar that uncork, kick, or feed our dreams are in fact less questionable than the everyday corkscrews, Eiffel Tower legs, and pieces of sugar which are so familiar that they become invisible and therefore non-existent."[5] There indeed lies the essence, the ease with which Man Ray transformed the most banal image or modest visual record into a source of "mystery."

This was the direction in which Breton attempted to prod Jacques-André Boiffard when he asked him to provide photographic illustrations for *Nadja* in 1928. The results are well known: Boiffard's pictures — perhaps hamstrung by overly strict instructions — remain uninterestingly banal. Man Ray, meanwhile, knew how to "paint" with the most modest photo; it might even be said without exaggeration that this was all he could do, given that his strictly painterly creativity was almost always destroyed by dismayingly impoverished technique.

An example can be found in his "mathematical equations," which yielded a series of photographs between 1934 and 1936 and a series of paintings some ten years

1) Man Ray, Self Portrait, *Boston : Little Brown, 1988, 97.*

2) Man Ray, Self Portrait *(1988), p.135.*

3) Man Ray, Self Portrait *(1988), p. 206*

4) Paul Hill and Thomas Cooper, *Dialog with Photography,* Thames & Hudson, *1979, p.9. Reprinted in* Camera *and in Philippe Sers,* Man Ray Photographe, *Paris, 1981, without crediting the interviewers.*

5) Rene Crevel, *"Le Miroir aux Objets,"* L'Art Vivant, *no 14-15, July 1925, p.24.*

Untitled, 1924

Élevage de Poussière [Dust Breeding], 1920

6) Christian Zervos, "Mathématiques et Art Abstrait,"
Cahiers d'Art, 1936, p.10.

later. There is no trace of his visit to the Institut Poincaré (leading to the suggestion that his interest was the result of a chance encounter with these physical models of mathematical formulas, rather than the encouragement of Duchamp or Max Ernst), but his interest is incontrovertible since, if Lucien Treillard is to be believed, he photographed them on various occasions between 1934 and 1936. Above all, he allowed the photos to be published in 1936 as illustration to a long article by Christian Zervos criticizing abstract art which "reduces art to the positioning of several squares and circles, [to] decorativeness in its lowliest form." [6]

Unfortunately, a small album of contact prints titled Contacts for *Shakespearian Equations*, acquired by the Musée National d'Art Moderne in 1994, sheds little light on the issue. Dated 1935-1948 on the back cover, it contains 31 contacts, many of which bear cropping indications as well as annotations such as a mathematical description by Michel Colinet, a title from Shakespeare, the letter "T" in red pencil (referring to a potential *tirage*, or print?), or occasional indications of dimensions. Sometimes the letter "C" is added in blue pencil, the meaning of which is obscure. Nothing indicates the purpose of this album : was it a series of "photographic notes" for a set of paintings, or a dummy of a small book of photographs ? What is revealing, however, is Man Ray's own discussion of the objects, for he indicates what it was that sparked his interest. It was not just the fantastic nature of these three-dimensional transcriptions of highly precise mathematical

7) *Man Ray, Self Portrait (1988), p. 291.*

8) *Man Ray, Self Portrait (1988), p. 291.*

9) *Zervos, p.6.*

10) *Umberto Eco, L'Oeuvre Ouverte, Paris : Le Seuil, 1965, p.123.*

11) *Eco, p.123.*

12) *See Emmanuelle de l'Ecotais, Le Fonds Photographique de la Dation Man Ray, étude et inventaire, PhD dissertation, Université de Paris IV (Sorbonne), 1997, pp. 170-171.*

equations (which would earn them a place in the Museum of Modern Art's 1934 Fantastic Art Show), but "the fact that they were man-made."[7] This meant the pictures he produced were not abstract, as Breton feared, because "all abstract art appeared to [Man Ray] as fragments : enlargements of details in nature and art, whereas these objects were complete microcosms."[8] Their shapes "are undeniably beautiful, often unpredictable, sometimes haunting, which draws them close to the shapes of art. But when they revert to their true nature ... these objects have absolutely no relationship to the irrational [element] inherent in art."[9] What pushes them into the artistic sphere, then, is the photographic image Man Ray produced, representing an approach that establishes these images as an extension of the photographs he did from 1918 onwards, such as *Man* and *Woman*, where photography was already being used as a tool for generating ambiguity, for revealing the fundamentally indeterminate nature of photographic reality. Man Ray enabled photography to participate in art's new-found freedom, namely the infinite power of unconscious, proliferating projections, spurring him to follow a path where discoveries were always highly unpredictable. In theory, then — as Umberto Eco has suggested — there might be a parallel between the development of non-Euclidean geometries and the abandonment of classical geometrical forms by fauvist and cubist artists, between the advent of abstract painting and the emergence in mathematics of imaginary numbers, transfinite numbers, and set theory."[10] As Eco notes, of course, one should be wary of the perils of a determinism which is now tending to replace the Marxist vulgate with a causality as absurd as it is illusory. Yet it remains true that "values once thought to be absolute, thought to constitute the metaphysical framework of the world" now appear, in the light of new scientific concepts, to be a question of convention. They are "no longer indispensable for explaining the world or for creating another one." When it comes to art, however, "it is less a question of finding rigorous formal equivalents for these new concepts than of negating old concepts. Here again one finds, alongside a science which promises nothing more than a supposed structure of things, an effort by art to give this new world an image that is at least plausible, an image that general sensibility — always lagging behind intellect — has not yet adopted."[11]

By overturning the conventions of perspective deemed intrinsic to the photographic process, beginning with his earliest "autonomous" experiments in the medium, Man Ray placed photography at the heart of the artistic debate of the day. Thanks to him, photography — an instantaneous and mechanical appropriation of reality — even became the ideal medium of surrealism. A photograph like the 1920 *Moving Sculpture*, for instance, does not seem like a simple depiction of sheets on a clothesline, but appears instead to answer Leonardo's question : how can the wind be painted?[12] This materialization of a "breath of air" tells us more about Man Ray's desire to free sculpture from materiality than it does about the primitive state of French society which willingly aired its laundry in public (as suggested by the caption "France" when this picture was published in the sixth issue of *La Révolution Surréaliste*, March 1, 1926).

Contrary to what might be thought, however, the dematerialization of photography was not linked to the use of new photographic processes. Attentive study of MNAM's Man Ray archives shows that special technical effects

Course d'Autos [Car Race], 1926

Contacts For Shakespearian [Sic], Equations, 1935-1948

(superimposition of negatives or screens, inversion, solarization, etc.), were more likely to be used in pictures of a professional nature, indicating their "artistic" status. Cropping was the only artifice that Man Ray employed consistently. Whether indicated in pencil, pen, or by folding the contact print, he constantly "de-realized his images" by cropping them.[13] What at first was probably a technical constraint dictated by his lack of adequate lighting and lenses, soon became a strength. "Some of the most effective photographs ... were magnifications of a detail of the face and body. .... I carried this idea further by giving such details a texture inherent in the medium itself, coarse grain, partial reversal of the negative and other technical variations; all frowned upon by straight photographers."[14]

Yet while it is true that several of his major images combined all these methods, their use was in no way mandatory in obtaining an effect of unreality. An example of this is his 1920 photograph of the "Large Glass" in Duchamp's New York studio. The feeble light level that forced him to open the aperture wide and make a long exposure, the apparent change in scale, and the tilting of the picture plane turned what could have been a banal reproduction of work-in-progress into a strange landscape in which the eye contrives to see dust and tufts of cotton either as a vast, cloudy expanse partly obscuring traces of unintelligible architecture, or as a sandy desert dotted with rocks and enigmatic ruins.

For Man Ray, photography freed painting from its role of anecdotal depiction. But painters still had to free photography from its strictly utilitarian role. With photography, he claimed, "we merely enlarged our scope, our vocabulary."[15]

Fifty years later, the lesson taught by Man Ray is still valid. Although one needs "a mirror and larks to hunt larks, mirroring the object alone will not suffice to charm. That is why photographers, like painters and poets, cannot be content with a meticulous account."

13) Of the 5,004 contact prints in the MNAM archives, 1,120 bear cropping indications, which corresponds fairly closely to the number of pictures actually used. Emmanuelle de l'Ecotais's analysis of the archives show that not a single negative was printed "full frame."

14) Man Ray, Self Portrait (1988), p. 206.

15) Man Ray, La Photographie Peut Etre de l'Art

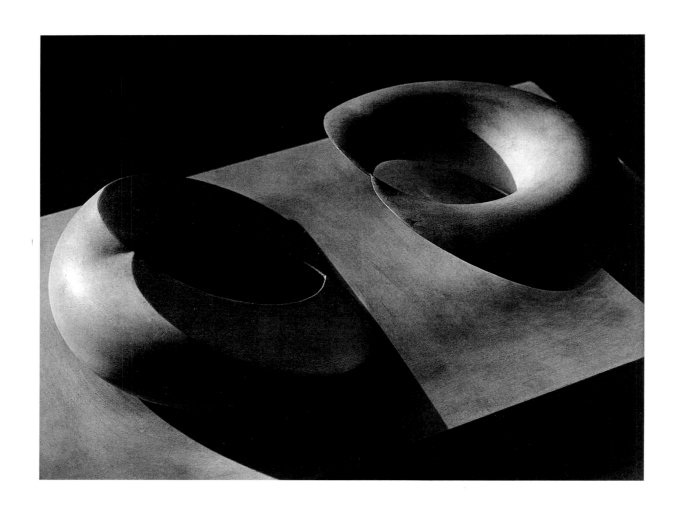

Objet Mathématique [Mathematical Object], 1934-1936

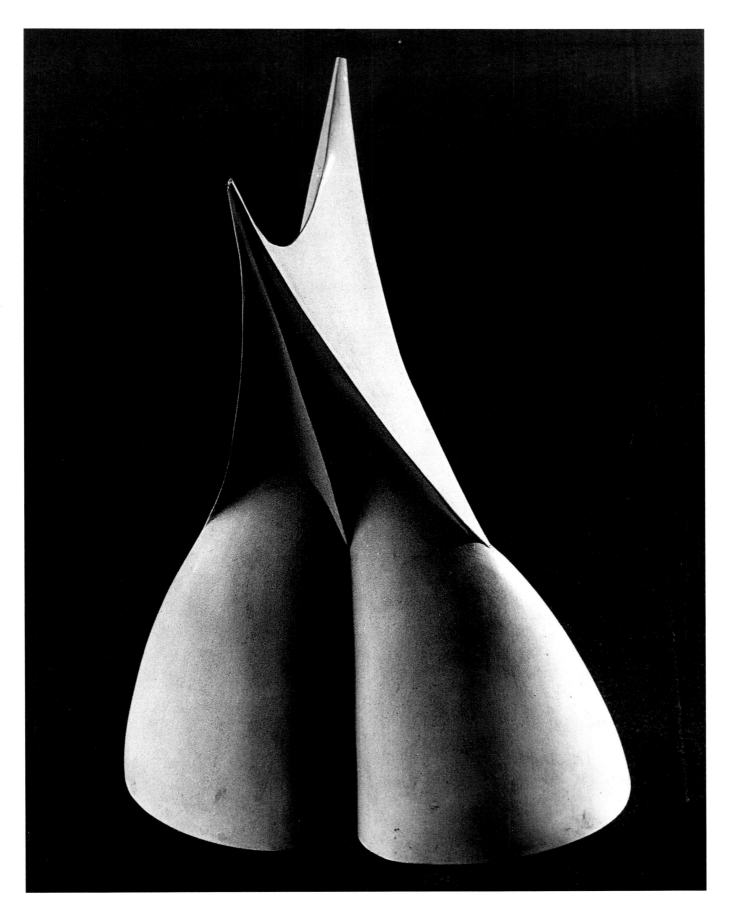

Objet Mathématique [Mathematical Object], 1934-1936

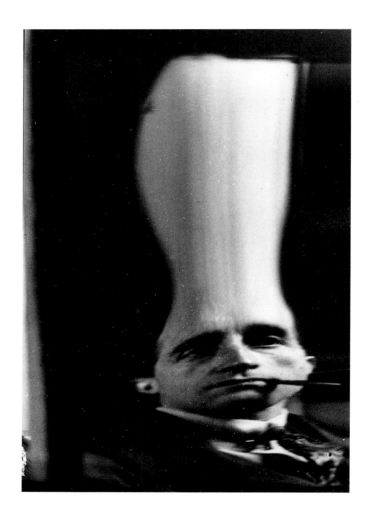

Marcel Duchamp, Distorsion [Marcel Duchamp Distorted], 1925

Moving Sculpture or *La France*, 1920

Portrait, circa 1930

Untitled, circa 1930

Marcel Duchamp, circa 1920

Interview with Lucien Treillard

Musée National d'Art Moderne (MNAM) : *When did you meet Man Ray?*

Lucien Treillard (L.T.) : At the time I was working for Georges Visat, who published editions of Max Ernst, Matta, etc. He sent me to see Man Ray because he wanted to do prints and books with him. So I went to Rue Férou and knocked on the door. That was in the early 1960s. Man Ray's dealer was Petithory. Man Ray received me cordially, and I went back more and more often, because he needed help — he was beginning to get old. There was a lot of physical handling in his studio : you had to climb up to the loft to get paintings, bring them down, hunt for negatives, and so on. I began working one hour a day, then two, then nine — it happened little by little.

At the time, Petithory was a bookseller and publisher — he was the one who published the treatise on *Mannequins*. When preparing his catalogues, he would delve into Man Ray's library, since he had saved nearly all his documents. He also took [Man Ray] on vacation, to the south of France and more or less everywhere.

Man Ray asked me to help him with editions of lithographs and engravings. Things were beginning to pick up, and it was more than he could handle. A Man Ray wasn't expensive — he was paid 3,000 francs for an edition of an object, it was pathetic. Arturo Schwarz manufactured the objects in Paris, and had Man Ray sign them before leaving for Italy again. Man Ray wasn't very satisfied ; he wanted to monitor the execution. He was demanding. I remember that he made me redo *N for Nothing*, a pretty simple object, five or six times, because the sandpaper was never glued just right. The simpler the object seemed, the trickier the execution turned out to be.

MNAM : *Was he demanding in terms of the technique required for an idea he had in mind, or in terms of an earlier version?*

L.T. : In terms of the idea as it had been originally materialized. He felt, for example, that Schwarz's executions were inadequate. When Zerbib and Marconi wanted to issue objects in silver, he thought it would betray the original works, which were in wood most of the time.

MNAM : *It was always in terms of the original work?*

L.T. : Or the photo of the original work, since very often the original work had been lost or destroyed. A lot were lost during the war, in particular at Rue du Val-de-Grâce, where Ady had remained long after Man Ray left for the United States.

An absolutely charming man, who had come back from Germany, moved in with her. She cared for him, fed him, and so on. Obviously, they had no source of income. The day they couldn't meet the rent, they simply walked out, taking everything in the studio, but not in the maid's room. The things in the cellar, two Mirós and Duchamp's *Bottle Rack*, were never found — which is understandable, since the Mirós were in wood and were probably used for firewood during the war, whereas Duchamp's *Bottle Rack* probably reverted to its original use.

Part of the collection of 1,500 negatives I have given to the museum comes directly from Man Ray ; the rest I bought from Ady's friend. He's still alive, although Ady herself died several years ago. When he wanted to sell his house on Rue Pascal, he sent me a note asking me to come over, and he showed me what he had saved. I acquired it all, except for the birds used for props in fashion photos, birds executed by J.-M. Frank, probably after a model by Giacometti.

MNAM : *And yet many negatives have been lost.*

L.T. : All the negatives were kept in the maid's room on Rue du Val-de-Grâce. Two people went into that room during the war : Eluard, who had the right to take works and sell them, in agreement with Man Ray, and Ady Fidelin's brother, who did not have the same respect for Man Ray's oeuvre and probably destroyed or sold the photos.

MNAM : *But he didn't sell negatives.*

L.T. : No, they were unsalable. But negatives are fragile — they were easily dispersed or broken. Man Ray told me that when he returned, a lot of them were in pieces on the floor.

MNAM : *When we made an inventory of the collection, we were amazed by the almost total absence of negatives of rayographs. No more than thirty exist, which is relatively few in terms of the two-hundred-odd that are listed. Yet a certain number of rayographs were re-photographed, notably for* Les Champs Délicieux.

L.T. : That's not all — there are many items for which the negatives have disappeared, like *Mannequins*, which Man Ray never found again. You only needed to have a box on a ledge of the maid's room, it could fall to the floor and get smashed.

MNAM : *So you think the destruction was random, rather than systematic?*

L.T. : Completely random. The only destruction intended by Man Ray concerned negatives of "clients." He broke a certain number of them himself, then one day he gave me an enormous box and a hammer, and he said, "Take that home and bust it up, there'll be too much broken glass, I don't want to see it around here." But now you have them [in the archives], and I think they have a certain interest.

MNAM : *What do you mean by "clients?"*

L.T. : People who came to his studio to be photographed, with their wives, children, and dogs. You have a whole stack of them, but he probably did ten times as many. Man Ray was a highly popular photographer. All the Americans who came to Paris wanted to sit for him.

When I first arrived at Rue Férou, the negatives were all filed in a back room, with names on the boxes. But some boxes were already ruined, because dampness had seeped under the emulsion. I remember a box of portraits of Kiki and another of Duchamp, which he had me print contacts from. Duchamp's face can barely be made out.

MNAM : *What's surprising is that, in the end, there are relatively few major pictures among the contact prints. There are stacks of portraits, but Man Ray's really important pictures don't exist in contacts, as though he worked directly on them. For instance, with an image like* Tears, *we have a full-frame contact of the entire head, but we don't have the cropping indications, which we know thanks to various vintage prints — one of just the two eyes, and one of a single, upside-down eye.*

L.T. : Pictures like those were largely composed in the darkroom, based on trial-and-error. It should be added that composition was often ignored when the photo was taken. There's a strong link between photographers' visual defects and what they produce.

MNAM : *What do you mean by that?*

L.T. : A photographer might be near-sighted or astigmatic, and Man Ray claimed that you could see it on the print.

In his case, since he didn't plan the final composition during the session, his subsequent work was one of cropping — cropping in pen or pencil as you have on the contacts, or cropping by cutting the negative, you have that too, and sometimes by taking the contact print and folding it. Those are basically the three

techniques he used. At that point, a difficulty arose when making the print : if you want a print of very fine quality — something that Gassman fully understood — you have to develop a system of masks because you can't use the standard system. You're obliged to do the masking by hand, which means that to get a high quality photo, a positive print, you have to produce ten that go straight into the garbage can. For a certain number of pictures, Gassman was very successful. Man Ray showed him how to proceed.

He wanted to reproduce the original framing and the atmosphere of the photograph as it had been at the outset. That's why I say that the contact prints are crucial, since they're the prints he made to have a quick view of what he'd shot, in order to choose the final image.

MNAM : *He nevertheless did a lot of work in the darkroom to produce his key images. If we take other examples, like the 1923* Nude Kiki, *it's an image that matured through darkroom work, work at the printing stage. He was not as lazy as he made out, that was just a pose he adopted.*

L.T. : He didn't function like the other artists he knew, like Braque and Picasso, who entered their studios at 8 a.m., left at noon, and started again at 2 p.m. He created when the spirit moved him, when he felt like it ; even when he had a commission, he had to be prodded to get it done. But when I accompanied him during shooting sessions, for photos of mannequins in front of the television, for instance, or the final De Sade portraits, which are his last photos, the composition required a great deal of preparation time — the lights were all carefully calculated, he was constantly intervening. Taking the photo was really work.

MNAM : *And when he was doing a portrait?*

L.T. : I think there were two different cases. I'll exclude the family portraits because, when he came to my place on Sundays — I'd bought him a Polaroid — he'd take portraits at great speed, just for fun. But getting a portrait just right was extremely tricky. When he left for vacation on the Basque coast, Boiffard would stay at his studio, where [Man Ray] had set up spot lights, the camera, all the equipment, and people had to sit at a precise spot. He gave Boiffard full instructions, as their letters confirm.

MNAM : *But Boiffard wasn't his assistant for very long.*

L.T.: After [Boiffard] left, he hired another assistant — he always had one. He hated carrying the plates and box cameras, which were very heavy. Even the Graflex was relatively heavy. Boiffard was useful, being very strong.

MNAM: *Even for his early exhibitions, Man Ray had someone do the printing?*

L.T.: Yes, he didn't print much. Jacqueline Goddard told me she'd seen him print two or three times, that's all. He made the contact prints, and on back of the contacts you have instructions for the assistant. He didn't touch a thing after that, he knew exactly what he wanted, all the technical information — format, paper, full instructions — were given to the assistant. He wanted to be as free as possible. He couldn't do everything, couldn't paint, build his objects, take care of his friends, go to surrealist meetings, do fashion photos. So it was his assistant who worked in the photo studio. That's why he always had a studio.

MNAM: *He did a lot of fashion work, but didn't do advertising, for example.*

L.T.: He did a few ad photos for jewelry, for necklaces, rings — fashion-related advertising. There were a few photos done for industrial furnaces and steel mills, there was *Electricité*, but it was on the fringe of commission work; he didn't need to do it to survive. At that time, he was the only one who was comfortably off — all the people I've met who knew him in the 1920s and '30s have told me that he was the only one who was financially secure. I forget who told me — Meret, maybe, or Jacqueline — that they all ran up bills at the cafés, whereas he always had the wherewithal to pay for his meals and drinks. It should be mentioned that he began doing fashion photography very early thanks to Yvonne Chastel and Elsa Schiaparelli, whom he met in New York in 1919. It's important since fashion paid best at the time.

MNAM: *It's true that there are fashion photographs published in 1924–1925. The oldest examples are the Poiret photos from 1922, but only two are known to exist. Above all, one gets the impression that the fashion business really took off with* Harper's Bazaar, *beginning only in 1934–1935.*

L.T.: That's because of economic conditions: France was in a crisis, whereas he was working for the American market, which was picking up again. He benefited from an advantageous situation. In the 1930s, America was in depression, but he was living in France. He was also able to build up a special clientele, and I think that special clientele continued to grow. Rich Americans began to visit France, and they all wanted to be photographed by Man Ray.

MNAM: *Strangely, he no longer profited from that situation in the 1950s.*

L.T.: He was no longer interested in photography at that point. He did a little in the United States, especially portraits of Juliet, as well as a few reproductions of paintings. But it was no longer his source of income. During the war, in the United States, he'd tried to sell his art work through exhibitions. When he returned to Paris, he wanted to come across as a painter, or a sculptor, or anything you like, but not a photographer; so he didn't do any more photography. He was interested in being recognized as an artist, not as a photographer. He wanted to forget that label.

At one point, he wanted to sell all his photographic material, the negatives along with the prints and the cameras. I think it was in 1961 when he made the first move. An American university was interested, but when he told them the price — he wanted $50,000 — they thought it was too much. He didn't pursue it, he thought it was unsalable.

MNAM: *Why did Man Ray begin re-printing photographs after the war?*

L.T.: The reprints from old negatives were the result of exhibition requests, which were increasing at that time, whereas he didn't have any old prints. In 1962, when the Bibliothèque Nationale gave him a retrospective, he had to ask Pierre Gassman to do the prints. He didn't have enough old prints, especially not of the major pictures that would give a true idea of his work.

MNAM: *Or the idea he wanted to give....*

L.T.: Or the idea he wanted to give of his work. Because when the negatives where chosen, he eliminated some things and selected others that he wanted reproduced. Moreover, like Duchamp, he wanted to see the same works reproduced over and over, which he thought was the best form of publicity. He was an American — pragmatic and efficient.

MNAM : *But how could he agree to release such mediocre prints, especially for exhibitions? Why didn't he print them himself?*

L.T. : In fact, Man Ray only printed his contacts. He always had an assistant. He couldn't have cared less about the quality of the final print, it didn't interest him — he was very pleased with the show at the BN in 1962.

MNAM : *He didn't like to print?*

L.T. : He always told me that when he found an assistant able to do things as well as he could, or better, he'd let him get on with it.

MNAM : *And yet you get the impression that he liked technical manipulations a lot, that there was a "craft" side to him.*

L.T. : There was a manual side to him, but it was for innovating, for installing a canopy in the studio, or inventing a swinging table so that he could have tea or read in bed. Whereas printing was always more or less the same thing.

MNAM : *Did he place more importance on old prints than on modern prints?*

L.T. : At first he was shocked that people only wanted old prints — at the time they were called "vintage." People always wanted vintage prints, without knowing exactly what the term covered; it might be a 1922 negative printed in 1938. This vagueness still exists today, for that matter, nurtured by dealers.

MNAM : *And what do you think? These days, people tend to think that Man Ray's original production is limited to the vintage prints, and that the modern versions, such as the prints done for Photokina in 1960, are only an approximation of the original work.*

L.T. : I find that modern prints lack the presence found in the old prints. Especially the contacts, which have a kind of aura.

MNAM : *Don't you think it's something we project onto those works — which are theoretically reproducible works — a mind-set which is always the same, related to the idea of a relic?*

L.T. : I don't think so. There's a quality to the image, there is also a deepness to the blacks, an aging, which is very lovely. The papers are different. Man Ray placed great importance on the paper for certain images. He conducted trials with Guilleminot, Kodak, Léonard and Agfa papers, and he used nearly transparent paper for certain portraits, rayographs, and *Noire et Blanche.* His papers were very handsome, often buff-colored, slightly tinted, and produced a richness, substance, that has been lost with modern papers, which are much too white.

MNAM : *So, according to you, the real difference between a print done in the 1960s and a vintage print is not whether Man Ray printed it himself or not, since clearly he didn't even do his own printing in the 1920s, instead it's the paper....*

L.T. : It's the object. The object isn't the same. When you hang them on the wall, there's not a moment's hesitation. I find the contact prints even richer. Man Ray made lots of small prints, for economic reasons — between 1920 and 1940 paper was expensive, as were darkroom materials, which explains the number of post cards he had in the studio, I'm convinced there were at least a thousand. Postcards were done on very handsome heavy paper or card, and he loved his prints on postcards, which he often did himself.

MNAM : *Postcards were also a good way of disseminating his images.*

L.T. : That's right. It should be said that at the time, between 1920 and 1940, the dissemination of his works was totally amazing. Publications in every European country made it possible to know what photographers were producing — his work was seen even in Japan and the United States. And Man Ray's prints are small format — although you have a large format rayograph in your collection, there are not many of them, because it's simpler to produce a rayograph by direct contact than by enlarging with a lateral light source.

MNAM : *Rayographs are another matter. It's true that there are few large-sized exhibition prints. Except for later shows like the ones at the BN and Photokina—and in the latter case it was at Grüber's request.*

L.T. : The pictures he exhibited, and which I know, are mostly rather small, glued to cardboard or to heavy large-format paper, as was fashionable at the time.

MNAM : *Because, unlike the Russians and Moholy-Nagy, he refused to make photography the equivalent of painting.*

L.T. : For him, photography was another medium which, like painting, allowed him to create art works. He was aware of this right from the early 1920s.

MNAM : *So he returned to photography only in the context of the exhibitions in the 1960s, and only in terms of his personal development.*

L.T. : He only took up photography again because the dealers encouraged him to. Photos were beginning to reach a public, to sell. The first pictures I saw bought by [Arnold] Crane went for $40, I think. Later, prices went up a little, going to $50, $60, $70. But Crane made purchases in installments. I remember that Man Ray had me stamp them [with one of the various studio stamps] and would say, "It's for Crane, just put any old stamp on it; don't bother asking me — whichever one you like." He enjoyed earning money, but he hated people who came solely for that. He dictated which pictures he'd sell, and slipped modern prints in. He jumbled up the prints, just like in the BN show.

MNAM : *So the conclusion is that dating cannot be reliably deduced from the studio stamp?*

L.T. : It's often very tricky. The problem of dating Man Ray's prints, as with almost every photographer, is highly complicated. The same goes for the dates written next to his signature. When he wrote "Man Ray Paris 1928," 1928 was often the date the photo was taken, not when the print was made. He did that often, though not systematically.

MNAM : *So you think that if he returned extensively to the field of photography in the 1960s, it was due to pressure from the context, from dealers?*

L.T. : When Crane arrived — who deserves credit for being one of the first American collectors after the war — he bought a lot from Man Ray, who said to himself that he could profit from it. Even at a modest price, the money added up. He also saw the attraction of working with Petithory : the *Traité des Mannequins* sold well. The same thing held for the Italians. So why not redo the photographs?

MNAM : *Especially when you have them redone by others, which is even easier.*

L.T. : When he produced the book *Voies Lactées* [*Milky Ways*], it was still photographic work even if it appeared in book form. He was highly interested in the problem of grays at the time. He was shocked by the photos he received, which were always in black and white. There was a point when it was totally black and white, which he found shocking. At that point, he wanted to do the white book on milky ways, therefore completely white,

since the typeface was white and white dominated in the photos, white and values of gray; he even did the three photos of Julie Lawson which are studies in gray. He really wanted to have gray images, with various values of gray. It was total experimentation.

MNAM : *Why wasn't he more interested in color?*

L.T. : He patented a color process, but it didn't have much success. He nevertheless used this transparent process to photograph all the celebrities of the day — Greco, Montand, Dominguez. The drawback was that it produced a unique work, painstakingly. Very few photographers of his generation were interested in color. Man Ray himself began with autochromes at an early date, in 1925; he also used a three-color system for the 1934 album. But reproducing colors was extremely difficult at the time. He also did some color photographs in California with the first Kodacolor film, which are rather successful. They're portraits of Juliet.

MNAM : *Let's talk about the rayographs. Tristan Tzara was known to have a collection of schadographs, and Tzara and Man Ray were pretty close.*

L.T. : Man Ray must have seen them. He didn't discover rayographs by chance. Schad's work was published in *Dadaphone*, he saw it, everyone saw it at the time. And then there was an explosion of photograms, everyone was doing them — they existed in Poland, Russia, in practically every country. So it is probable that he was aware of Schad's work. It's also significant that Tzara, who owned some schadographs, wrote the preface to *Champs Délicieux* and helped launched rayographs. But [Man Ray] always denied it, because he wanted to present a certain image of his oeuvre. There's an enormous difference between rayographs and schadographs. They don't occupy the same universe, they don't use the technique in the same way — Man Ray worked in the darkroom, which was not the case with Schad.

MNAM : *The same problem arises with solarization, because there are two stories : in the first, Man Ray says that the door to the studio opened accidentally, while in the second Lee Miller says that a mouse ran under her feet, startling her, and that she turned on the light. Which version is true?*

L.T. : I haven't a clue. Lee always told me that she was the one who turned on the light, and that she showed the outcome to

Man Ray, who found it very beautiful and began to systematize it.

MNAM : *So she really stuck to her version?*

L.T. : Don't forget that Lee Miller, often presented as a complete beginner, was the daughter of a photographer and was already familiar with the technique ; she came to Paris to perfect her skills with Man Ray. They worked together on many pictures — there's perhaps a topic of research on what is due to one and what is due to the other, if it can be done.

MNAM : *Is it conceivable that unknown photographic works by Man Ray still exist, or do you think it's totally impossible?*

L.T. : When I was working with him, I'd find boxes of negatives and he'd say, "I never printed that one ; do it, and let's see what turns up." And some pictures appeared that way, which are not without interest, but for which he had never made a contact print. It's possible you'll find things that have never been printed in the collection now in your hands. Even I didn't do it systematically. But remember that in most cases, he would have cropped the image.

MNAM : *Not because he thought the images were uninteresting, but simply because circumstances led him to overlook them?*

L.T. : He just took a look at them against the light, and since they didn't interest him at that very moment....

MNAM : *And when he went back to his photogrphy in the 1960s....*

L.T. : He made a very precise selection of images that he thought were important and that he wanted to show. It was at that point that he set aside the things he wanted me to reproduce, and which appeared in his exhibitions.

MNAM : *But that was in terms of an image of the published work, not in terms of his collection of negatives.*

L.T. : A more complete image could perhaps be given, which would not be his personal selection. There are interesting images that you have in the archive of negatives, which he put aside, neglected, and which were never reproduced.

MNAM : *Wasn't his selection ultimately highly subjective? When you see, for example, the number of post-war pictures of Juliet, doesn't it ultimately skew the image of his overall production?*

L.T.. : Absolutely, but that corresponds to his output in America, where he only took pictures of Juliet. There are at least 200 of them. She was his only model. He also photographed the Heytum family. But he met lots of other people he didn't photograph — Calder, Richter, and so on.

MNAM : *He didn't take pictures of them the way he had of the surrealists.*

L.T. : That's right. He photographed Copley, took pictures of Arthur Miller, and Charlotte Heytum and her husband, but it was highly limited. In California, he no longer wanted to take photographs, he wanted to draw and paint. He took photos almost by chance ; on the other hand, he produced rayographs — you now have one — that I find very interesting.

MNAM : *But he didn't do many.*

L.T. : No, maybe ten or so. Not all of them have been catalogued, for that matter. Remember that he no longer had a studio in California — he was forced to go to an outside darkroom to work. And back in Paris, he practically never used the darkroom on Rue Férou. He no longer had an assistant, and would constantly call on outside labs — Pierre Gassman, Serge Beguier when he lived on Rue de la Chaise, and that's all. The darkroom at Rue Férou went unused — the rain came in, he tried to protect the premises so that things wouldn't be ruined, but photography no longer interested him after he returned to Paris. He wanted to be recognized as an artist at last, not as a photographer.

Biography Man Ray (Emmanuel Radnitzky, called Man Ray)

1890 Born in Philadelphia, Pennsylvania, on August 20.

1911 Lived in New York, frequented Alfred Stieglitz's Gallery 291.

1912 Moved to Ridgefield, New Jersey.

1913 Discovered Marcel Duchamp's work at the Armory Show. Met the Belgian-born poetess Adon Lacroix, whom he married in May.

1915 Published *The Ridgefield Gazook*, a four-page pamphlet in the Dada spirit. Met Marcel Duchamp. Executed his first photographic reproductions for the catalogue of his show at the Daniel Gallery (October-November). Moved back to New York.

1916 First portrait photos.

1917 First airbrush work. First cliché-verre.

1918 *Man* and *Woman*.

1920 Founded the Société Anonyme with Marcel Duchamp and Katherine Dreier. Photographed part of Duchamp's "Large Glass," a photo that Duchamp later titled *Élevage de Poussière* [Dust Breeding].

1921 First work exhibited at a photography show, the 15th Annual Exhibition of Photographs, in Philadelphia (March 7–26). Published the sole issue of *New York Dada* (April) with Duchamp. Sent two photographs, *L'Homme* and *La Femme*, to the Paris show called *Salon Dada : Exposition Internationale* (June 6–30). Arrived in Paris on July 22. First stayed in the same hotel as Tristan Tzara, Hôtel de Boulainvilliers, then moved in August to a room in the apartment of Yvonne Chastel and Marcel Duchamp at 22 Rue de la Condamine. Began to photograph reproductions of paintings for artists, finishing the sessions by doing a portrait. Met Adrienne Monnier, who had him do portraits of the writers she published. In December, took a room at the Grand Hôtel des Ecoles on Rue Delambre, which he turned into a small photographic studio. Met Alice Prin, known as Kiki of Montparnasse. The

Exposition Dada Man Ray show was held at Librarie Six (December 3-31).

1922 Jean Cocteau published an "Open Letter to Monsieur Man Ray, American Photographer," concerning the rayographs, in *Les Feuilles Libres* (April–May). Man Ray's portraits of artists and writers were published in *Vanity Fair* (June). Success as a portrait photographer enabled him to move to a veritable studio at 31 bis, Rue Campagne-Première, in July. The October issue of *Littérature* published *Dust Breeding* (under the title, *Voici le domaine de Rrose Sélavy – Comme il est aride – Comme il est fertile – Comme il est joyeux – Comme il est triste*). Published his album *Champs Délicieux* in December, with a preface by Tristan Tzara.

1923 Hired Berenice Abbott as his assistant, which she would remain until 1926. Made his first film, *The Return to Reason*, first shown on July 6 during a Dada performance called *Le Coeur à Barbe* at the Théâtre Michel. In December, moved to the Hôtel Istria at 29 Rue Campagne-Première, the studio at number 31 bis being henceforth devoted exclusively to his photography.

1924 The June issue (no. 13) of *Littérature* published his *Violon d'Ingres*. Began to work for *Vogue* (English, French and American editions) in July. Article on Man Ray by Robert Desnos in *Paris-Journal* on December 14.

1925 Georges Ribemont-Dessaignes published an article on "Man Ray" in *Les Feuilles Libres* (no. 40, May/June). Photographed the "Pavillon de l'Élégance" for *Vogue* (published in the French and English editions in August, in the American edition in September).

1926 The Galerie Surréaliste opened with *Tableaux de Man Ray et Objets des Iles* (March 26-April 10). Published *Noire et Blanche* in *Vogue* (French edition, May). Made the film *Emak Bakia* (first shown at the Théâtre du Vieux Colombier on November 23). Presented his rayographs at the *International Exhibition of Modern Art Assembled by*

the Société Anonyme at the Brooklyn Museum (November 19, 1926 – January 1, 1927).

1927 Voyage to New York for his *Recent Painting and Photographic Compositions* show at the Daniel Gallery (February – April).

1928 Worked for the magazine *Vu*, only occasionally for *Vogue*. Participated in the *Exposition Surréaliste* at the Sacre du Printemps gallery (April 2 – 15) and in the Salon des Indépendants de la Photographie (called the Salon de l'Escalier) at the Théâtre des Champs-Élysées. Made the film *Étoile de Mer*, which premiered at the Studio des Ursulines on May 13.

1929 In January, filmed *Les Mystères du Château de Dé* in the villa of the count and countess de Noailles in Hyères. The Arts Club of Chicago hosted *Photographic Compositions by Man Ray* (February 5–19). Participated in the Stuttgart show, *Internationale Ausstellung des Deutschen Werkbunds, Film und Foto* (May 18 – July 7). Met Lee Miller, who worked as his assistant until 1932. Took a studio at 8 Rue du Val-de-Grâce. Discovered solarization. Show of *Tableaux and Derniers Rayogrammes* at the Galerie des Quatre-Chemins (November 2–14).

1930 The first monograph on Man Ray was written by Georges Ribemont-Dessaignes and published by Gallimard.

1931 Produced an advertising booklet for the Paris Electricity Board, *Electricité*, with a preface by Pierre Bost. The Galerie Alexandre III in Cannes hosted *Photographies de Man Ray* (April 13–19), with a catalogue preface by Francis Picabia. The October issue of *Art et Médicine* published his photographs of Paris.

1932 Participated in the *Surrealist Exhibition* at the Julien Levy Gallery in New York. Photographed the French can-can dancer Lydia, whose make-up inspired his photograph, *Tears*.

1933 Worked for the magazine *Minotaure*,

which published his text "L'Age de la Lumière" (*Minotaure*, no. 3/4). During the summer, joined Duchamp, Gala, and Dalí in Cadaqués, and photographed Gaudí's architecture in Barcelona.

1934   James Thrall Soby published *Photographs by Man Ray 1920 – Paris 1934*, with texts by Tristan Tzara, Paul Eluard, André Breton, and Rrose Sélavy (Marcel Duchamp). Participated in the *Minotaure* show at the Palais des Beaux-Arts in Brussels (May 12 – June 3).

1934-1936   Discovered and photographed mathematical objects at the Institut Poincaré.

1935   Published "On Photography" in *Commercial Art and Industry* (vol. XVII, no. 104, February). First fashion photographs published in *Harper's Bazaar* in March. Produced the images for Paul Eluard's *Facile*. Published "Sur le Réalisme Photographique" in *Cahiers d'Art* (no. 5/6, text translated from English by Eluard).

1936   Met Adrienne Fidelin (known as Ady). Participated in the *Cubism and Abstract Art* show at the Museum of Modern Art in New York (March 2– April 19).

Moved to Rue Denfert-Rochereau. Bought a house in Saint-Germain-en-Laye. Spent the summer in Mougins with Picasso, Dora Maar, Nusch and Paul Eluard, Roland and Valentine Penrose. Showed his photographs of *Mathematical Objects* and his rayographs at the exhibition of *Fantastic Art, Dada, Surrealism* at the Museum of Modern Art in New York (December 7, 1936 – January 17, 1937).

1937   Rented an apartment in Antibes, and devoted himself entirely to painting. Published *La Photographie n'est pas l'Art* (Paris : GLM).

1938   Participated in the *Exposition Internationale du Surréalisme* at the Galerie des Beaux-Arts in Paris, photographing all the dummies on display.

1940   During the summer, left Paris for Lisbon, where he sailed for New York. Moved to Hollywood, California in July. Met Juliet Browner.

1944   Last pictures published by *Harper's Bazaar*. Took few photographs, except for portraits of Juliet and friends. The Pasadena Art Institute presented

Man Ray : Retrospective Exhibition, 1913 to 1944 (September 19 – October 29).

1946   Married Juliet. Met Bill Copley.

1948   Painted the *Shakespearian Equations* series, based on his photographs of mathematical objects.

1951   Returned permanently to Paris with Juliet in March. First lived at 5 Rue Jules-Chaplin, then moved in September to 2 bis Rue Férou (official declaration of change of residence dated September 7), where he remained until his death.

1961   Awarded Gold Medal for Photography at the Venice Biennial.

1962   The Bibliothèque Nationale in Paris organized *Man Ray, l'Oeuvre Photographique*, comprising 76 items, including four clichés-verre, 55 photographs, and two albums (*Champs Délicieux* and *Electricité*).

1963   Published his autobiography, *Self Portrait* (Boston : Little, Brown).

1966   *Man Ray* exhibition at the Los Angeles County Museum of Art.

1976   Died in Paris on November 18.

Solo Exhibitions which Included Photographs

1921   *Exposition Dada Man Ray*, Librarie Six, Paris, December 3–31 (2 photographs).

1926   *Tableaux de Man Ray et Objets des Iles*, Galerie Surréaliste, March 26 – April 10 (4 photographs).

1927   *Recent Painting and Photographic Compositions by Man Ray*, Daniel Gallery, New York, February – April.

1929   *Photographic Compositions by Man Ray*, The Arts Club of Chicago, Chicago, February 5–19.

Tableaux et Derniers Rayogrammes, Galerie des Quatre-Chemins, November 2–14.

1931   *Exposition de Photographies par Man Ray*,

Galerie Alexandre III, April 13–19.

1932   *Photographs by Man Ray*, Julien Levy Gallery, New York, April 9–30.

L'Exposition Man Ray, Oeuvres 1919–1932, Chez Dacharry, Paris, began November 25.

Oeuvres Récentes de Man Ray, Galerie Vignon, Paris, December 2–15.

1934   *An Exhibition of Photography by Man Ray*, Lund Humphries & Co., London, November 22 – December 8.

1935   *Man Ray Photographs*, Lund Humphries & Co., London, December 5–15.

Photographs and rayographs, Wadsworth Atheneum, Hartford, Conn.

Photographs and drawings, The Art Center School, Los Angeles, Ca.

1936   Valentine Dudensing Galleries, New York.

1937   *Les Dessins de Man Ray*, Galerie Jeanne-Bucher, Paris, November 5–20 (photographic enlargement of details of drawings).

1938   *Drawings and Photographs by Man Ray*, The Art Center School, Los Angeles, Ca.

1941   *Man Ray : Exhibition of Paintings, Watercolors, Drawings, Photographic Compositions*, Frank Perls Gallery, Hollywood, Ca., March 1–26.

1944   *Man Ray : Retrospective Exhibition 1913 to 1944*, The Pasadena Art Institute,

Pasadena, Ca., September 19 – October 29.

1948　*Man Ray*, Copley Galleries, Beverly Hills, Ca., December 14 – January 9.

1962　*Man Ray : l'Oeuvre Photographique*, Bibliothèque Nationale, Paris, May 22 – July 13.

1963　*Man Ray : Paintings, Drawings, Watercolors, Etcetera*, Cordier & Ekstrom, Inc., New York, April 30 – May 18.

1964　*Man Ray : Oggetti del mio Affetto*, Galleria Schwarz, Milan, March 14 – April 3 (one photograph).

1966　*Man Ray : Retrospective Exhibition 1908 –1965*. Los Angeles County Museum of Art, Los Angeles, Ca. (8 photographs).

1969　*Man Ray*, Studio Marconi, Milan, April – May (5 photographs).

　　　Man Ray, Galleria Il Fauno, Turin, October 13 – November 3.

1970　*Man Ray, A Selection of Paintings*, Cordier & Ekstrom, Inc., New York, January 14 – February 7 (one photograph).

　　　Man Ray, Photographs & Rayographs, Noah Goldowsky Gallery, New York, November 21 – December 21.

1971　*Man Ray, Photographs & Rayographs, Retrospective Exhibition*, Harry Lunn Gallery, Washington, D.C., October 16 – November 8.

　　　Man Ray : Duecentoventi Opere 1912–1971, Galleria Milano, Milan, June – September.

　　　Man Ray, Boymans–Van Beuningen Museum, Rotterdam, September 24 – November 7, 1971 ; Musée National d'Art Moderne, Paris, January 7 – February 28, 1972 ; Louisiana Museum, Humblebaek, Denmark, March – April 1972.

1972　*Man Ray : 40 Rayographies*, Galerie des Quatre-Movements, February 25 – March 25.

　　　Man Ray, Gissi Galleria d'Arte, Turin ; Galerie Françoise-Tournie, Paris, November 7 – December 15 ; Galleria dell'Arte Libreria Pictogramma, Rome.

1973　*Man Ray Opera Grafica*, Galleria Il

Collezionista d'Arte Contemporanea, Rome, October 24 – December 8.

Man Ray Photo Graphics from the Collection of Arnold H. Crane, Milwaukee Art Center, Wisc., February 10 – March 11.

1974　*Man Ray*, The Mayor Gallery, London.

　　　Man Ray, l'Intervenzione Fotografica, Galleria Il Fauno, Turin, April.

　　　Man Ray, Iolas Gallery, New York, May – June.

　　　Man Ray, Galerie Alexander Iolas, Paris, October.

　　　Man Ray, Galeria Iolas-Velasco, Madrid (9 photographs).

　　　Man Ray, Exposition Rétrospective 1913– 1973, Galerie Alexandra-Monett, Brussels, October – November.

1975　*Man Ray*, Der Spiegel Gallerie, Cologne, January.

　　　Man Ray, L'Occhio e il suo Doppio, Palazzo delle Esposizioni, Rome, July – September.

　　　Man Ray, Designi, Tempere, Fotografie e Oggetti, Galleria Dell'Oca, Rome, July 16 – October 10.

1976　*Man Ray*, Artcurial–Centre d'Art Plastique Contemporain, Paris, May 8 – July 19.

　　　Man Ray, l'Immagine Fotografica, Venice Biennial, San Giorgio, Venice, July 18 – October 10.

1977　*Man Ray, Photographies des Années 20 et 30*, American Cultural Center, Paris, May 17 – June 30.

1979　*Man Ray, Inventionen und Interpretationen*, Steinernes Haus am Romberge, Frankfurter Kunstverein, Frankfurt, October 14 – December 23, 1979 ; Kunsthalle, Basel, January 20 – February 24, 1980.

1980　*Man Ray, Photographs and Objects*, Birmingham Museum of Art, Alabama, February 1 – March 9 ; Columbia Museum of Art, South Carolina, April 13 – May 25 ; Columbus Museum of Art, Ohio, June 22 – August 3 ; Hunter Museum of Art, Chattanooga, Tennessee, September 7 – October 19.

1981　*Man Ray*, Knoedler Gallery, London, December.

　　　Man Ray, Musée National d'Art Moderne, Centre Georges Pompidou, Paris, December 10, 1981 – April 12, 1982.

　　　Man Ray, Objects and Photographs, Seibu Museum of Modern Art, Takanawa, November 9, 1981 – March 11, 1982.

1982　*Man Ray, Publications & Transformations*, Zabriskie Gallery, New York, February 10 – March 13 ; Meredith Long & Co., Texas, April 6 – May 1.

　　　Man Ray et ses Amis, Galerie Marion-Meyer, Paris, February 23 – April 3.

　　　Man Ray, Assemblages, Dipinti, Fotografie, Disegni dal 1912 al 1972, Galleria d'Arte Niccoli, Parma.

　　　Man Ray Foto's 1916 – 1975, Boymans-Van Beuningen Museum, Rotterdam, May 22 – July 5.

　　　Atelier Man Ray, Musée National d'Art Moderne, Centre Georges Pompidou, December 2, 1982 – January 23, 1983.

1983　*Man Ray*, Centre d'Art Contemporain, Rouen, March 4 – 26.

　　　Man Ray, Mathematical Objects, Still Life Photographs from 1936, Robert Miller Gallery, New York, May 3 – June 30.

　　　Man Ray Photografies, Galeria Eude, Barcelona, May.

　　　Man Ray, Care Varie e Variabili, Padiglione d'Arte Contemporanea, Milan, December 1, 1983 – January 9, 1984.

　　　Man Ray Photographe, Maison des Jeunes et de la Culture, Dole, December 10, 1983 – February 28, 1984.

1984　*Man Ray*, Odakyu Gallery, Tokyo, August 10–22, 1984 ; Museum of Modern Art, Kamakura, January 26 – February 24, 1985 ; Regional Art Museum, Shiga, March 2 – April 7, 1985 ; Regional Art Museum, Mië, April 13 – May 12, 1985 ; Navio Museum, Osaka, May 24 – June 18, 1985.

1985　*Man Ray, Objects of My Affection*, Zabriskie Gallery, New York January 23 – February 23.

Man Ray Fotograf, Centar Za Fotografiju, Film i Televisiju, Zagreb, February 7–27 ; Musej Savremene Umetnosti, Belgrade, March 3 – 28.

Man Ray Photographien, Wolfgang Gurlitt Museum, Linz, February 21 – April 8.

Uit het Atelier van Man Ray, Gemmentelijk van Reekum-museum, Apeldorn, Holland, June 22 – August 18.

Man Ray Designi, Museo Regionale di Palazzo Bellomo, Syracuse, Sicily, June 29 – July 28 (6 photographs).

Man Ray, Light Gallery, New York, October – November.

1986 *Cafe Man Ray*, G. Ray Hawkins Gallery, Los Angeles, Ca., January.

Man Ray : Fotografi, Rayogram, Tecniga, Objekt, Grafic, Kontshall, Lunds, June 7 – August 31.

Man Ray, Centre d'Action Culturelle, Saint-Brieuc, July 2 – August 29.

Man Ray, Nus, Galerie Octant, Paris, November 19 – December 19.

Man Ray, Galleria Vivita, Florence, December 13, 1986 – February 28, 1987 (2 photographs).

1987 *Man Ray*, Levy Gallerie, Hamburg, September 21 – October 30.

Man Ray, Seoul Gallery, Seoul, December 5, 1987 – January 1, 1988.

1988 *Man Ray : Photographien, Filme, frühe Objekte*, Schweizerische Stiftung für die Photographie, Kunsthaus, Zurich, March 12 – May 23.

Man Ray, Musée Municipal, Saint-Dié, March 12 – April 10.

Perpetual Motif, The Art of Man Ray, National Museum of American Art, Washington, D.C., December 2, 1988 – February 20, 1989 ; The Museum of Contemporary Art, Los Angeles, Ca., March 17 – May 28, 1989 ; The Menil Collection, Houston, Tx., June 30 – September 17, 1989 ; Museum of Contemporary Art, Philadelphia, Pa., October 14, 1989 – January 7, 1990.

1989 *Man Ray's Paris Portraits : 1921 – 1939*, Middendorf Gallery, Washington, D.C.

Man Ray Portraits, Zeit-Foto Salon, Tokyo, March 10 – 31.

Man Ray "360 Degrés de Liberté," Trianon de Bagatelle, Paris, March 28 – June 5.

Man Ray, l'Età delle Luci, Galleria Civica, Modena, October 29, 1989 – January 7, 1990.

1990 *Cent Ans de Man Ray*, Musée de l'Elysée, Lausanne, February 15 – April 1.

Man Ray, "Cent Anni de Libertà," Palazzo Fortuny, Venice, July 7 – August 26.

Man Ray, Derrière la Façade, Rencontres Internationales de la Photographie, Arles, August.

Man Ray, Bazaar Years : A Fashion Retrospective, International Center of Photography Midtown, New York, September 7 – November 25 ; Sala de Exposiciones del Circulo de Bellas Artes, Madrid, April 29 – June 23, 1991 ; Musée des Arts de la Mode et du Textile, Paris, October 14, 1992 – January 31, 1993.

Man Ray, Galerie Sona Zanettacci, Geneva, September 13 – October 16.

Man Ray 1890 – 1976, Sezon Museum of Art, Tokyo, September 29 – November 4, 1990 ; Tsukashin Hall, Amagasaki, November 10 – December 16, 1990 ; Tenjin Daimaru, Fukuoka, March 14–26, 1991 ; Museum of Art, Yokohama, April 6 – May 8, 1991 ; Daimaru Museum, Kyoto, August 15–20, 1991 ; Gobankan Seibu Akarenga Hall, Sapporo, August 31 – September 23, 1991.

1992 *Portraits Photographiques de Man Ray*, Musée Municipal, Orange, May 27 – June 30.

1993 *Man Ray et les Femmes*, Galerie 15, Paris, February 4 – March 27.

Cinéma, Exposition et Projection des Films de Man Ray, Festival du Cinéma Américain, Deauville, September 2–14 (2 photographs).

1994 *Man Ray 1890 – 1976*, Ronny Van de Velde Gallery, Antwerp, September 18 – December 18.

Man Ray Neues wie Vertrautes, Fotografien 1919–1949, Kunst Museum, Wolfsburg, October 8, 1994 – January 15, 1995.

1995 *Man Ray*, Serpentine Gallery, London, January 18 – March 12.

Man Ray Fotografia, Instituto Leones de Cultura, León, September 6 – October 1.

Man Ray, Sala de Exposiciones de la Diputación de Huesca, Huesca, December.

Man Ray, La Construzione dei Sensi, Galleria d'Arte Moderna e Contemporanea, Turin, October 5 1995 – January 7, 1996.

1996 *Man Ray*, Centre Photographique d'Ile-de-France, Pontault-Combault, June 12 – July 28.

Man Ray Fotografias, Museo Rufino Tamayo, Mexico, September.

Man Ray, Kunsthaus Wien, Vienna, September 19, 1996 – January 26, 1997.

Man Ray : Paris–LA, Robert Berman Gallery, Santa Monica, Ca., September 21, 1996 – January 31, 1997.

Man Ray : Photographic Retrospective 1917–1975, Station Gallery, Tokyo, October 20 ; Umeda Daimaru Museum, Osaka, October 29 – November 11 ; Daimaru Museum, Kyoto, April 3–15, 1997.

Man Ray at Rue Férou 1951–1997, Zabriskie Gallery, New York, October 29, 1996 – January 4, 1997.

Man Ray of My Affection (Teruo Ishihara Collection), City Art Museum, Nagoya, December 1–25.

1997 *Man Ray, Rétrospective 1912–1976*, Musée d'Art Moderne et d'Art Contemporain, Nice, February 22 – June 9.

List of Illustrations

Page 95 *Blanc et Noir* [White and Black], circa 1929
Solarized gelatin silver print
10.7 x 6.7 cm — 4 1/4" x 2 3/4"
Man Ray Estate Settlement, 1994
Mnam/Cci, Centre Georges Pompidou
AM 1994-394/2350

Page 96 *Chevelures* [Hair], 1937
Gelatin silver contact print made from the
original negative by
Jacques Faujour and Daniel Valet in 1998
Man Ray Estate Settlement, 1994
Mnam/Cci, Centre Georges Pompidou

Chevelures [Hair], 1937
Gelatin silver contact print made from the
original negative by
Jacques Faujour and Daniel Valet in 1998
Man Ray Estate Settlement, 1994
Mnam/Cci, Centre Georges Pompidou

Page 97 *Kiki*, circa 1925
Gelatin silver contact print made from the
original negative by
Jacques Faujour and Daniel Valet in 1998
Man Ray Estate Settlement, 1994
Mnam/Cci, Centre Georges Pompidou

Page 98 *Le Baiser* [The Kiss], circa 1932
Gelatin silver print
10.9 x 8.2 cm — 4 1/4" x 3 1/4"
Private collection, Paris

Page 99 *Ady and Nusch*, 1937
Gelatin silver print
11 x 8.3 cm — 4 1/2" x 3 1/4"
Man Ray Estate Settlement, 1994
Mnam/Cci, Centre Georges Pompidou
AM 1994-394/857

Page 100 *Lee Miller*, circa 1930
Gelatin silver print
8.2 x 5.2 cm — 3 1/4" x 2"
Man Ray Estate Settlement, 1994
Mnam/Cci, Centre Georges Pompidou
AM 1994-394/2043

Page 101 *Lee Miller*, circa 1930
Gelatin silver print
8.9 x 5.8 cm — 3 1/2" x 2 1/4"
Private collection, Paris

Lee Miller [Breasts], circa 1930
Gelatin silver print
13.8 x 23 cm
Galleria Nazionale d'Arte Moderna, Rome

Lee Miller, circa 1930
Gelatin silver print
8.4 x 5.8 cm — 3 1/4" x 2 1/4"
Man Ray Estate Settlement, 1994
Mnam/Cci, Centre Georges Pompidou
AM 1994-394/2024

Lee Miller, circa 1930
Gelatin silver print
8.2 x 5.7 cm — 3 1/4" x 2 1/4"
Man Ray Estate Settlement, 1994
Mnam/Cci, Centre Georges Pompidou
AM 1994-394/2023

Page 102 *Meret Oppenheim*, 1933
Gelatin silver print
6.1 x 4.2 cm — 2 1/2" x 1 3/4"
Man Ray Estate Settlement, 1994
Mnam/Cci, Centre Georges Pompidou
AM 1994-394/4400

Page 103 *Meret Oppenheim*, 1933
Gelatin silver print
6.2 x 8.3 cm — 2 1/2" x 3 1/4"
Man Ray Estate Settlement, 1994
Mnam/Cci, Centre Georges Pompidou
AM 1994-394/4399

Self-Portrait with Meret Oppenheim, 1933
Gelatin silver print
6 x 4.3 cm — 2 1/2" x 1 3/4"
Man Ray Estate Settlement, 1994
Mnam/Cci, Centre Georges Pompidou
AM 1994-394/4405

Self-Portrait with Meret Oppenheim, 1933
Gelatin silver print
6 x 4.5 cm — 3 1/2" x 1 3/4"
Man Ray Estate Settlement, 1994
Mnam/Cci, Centre Georges Pompidou
AM 1994-394/4394

Page 104 *Suzy Solidor*, 1929
Gelatin silver print
29.5 x 22.6 cm — 11 3/4" x 9"
The Museum of Modern Art, New York
Gift of James Thrall Soby

Suzy Solidor, 1929
Gelatin silver print
8.3 x 5.6 cm — 3 1/4" x 2 1/4"
Man Ray Estate Settlement, 1994
Mnam/Cci, Centre Georges Pompidou
AM 1994-394/1358

Suzy Solidor, 1929
Solarized gelatin silver print
8.5 x 5.8 cm — 3 1/4" x 2 1/4"
Man Ray Estate Settlement, 1994
Mnam/Cci, Centre Georges Pompidou
AM 1994-394/1364

Page 105 *Suzy Solidor*, 1929
Solarized gelatin silver print
8.6 x 5.8 cm — 3 1/2" x 2 1/4"
Man Ray Estate Settlement, 1994
Mnam/Cci, Centre Georges Pompidou
AM 1994-394/1357

Page 106 Nude, circa 1935
Gelatin silver print
10.4 x 6.4 cm — 4" x 2 1/2"
Man Ray Estate Settlement
Mnam/Cci, Centre Georges Pompidou
AM 1994-394/2361

Page 108 Kiki, circa 1926
Gelatin silver contact print made from the
original negative by
Jacques Faujour and Daniel Valet in 1998
Man Ray Estate Settlement, 1994
Mnam/Cci, Centre Georges Pompidou

Page 109 Kiki, 1926
Gelatin silver print
23.2 x 17.9 cm — 9 1/4" x 7"
Ludwig Museum, Cologne

Page 110 *Edward James*, 1937
Gelatin silver print
22.6 x17 cm — 9" x 6 3/4"
Sylvio Perlstein Collection, Antwerp

Page 111 *Edward James*, 1937
Gelatin silver print
9.1 x 7.1 cm — 3 1/2" x 2 3/4"
Man Ray Estate Settlement, 1994
Mnam/Cci, Centre Georges Pompidou
AM 1994-394/777

Edward James, 1937
Gelatin silver print
9.1 x 7.1 cm — 3 1/2" x 2 3/4"
Man Ray Estate Settlement, 1994
Mnam/Cci, Centre Georges Pompidou
AM 1994-394/783

Page 112 *Marcel Duchamp*, 1930
Solarized gelatin silver print
22.5 x 17 cm — 8 3/4" x 6 3/4"
The Museum of Modern Art, New York
Gift of James Thrall Soby

Page 113 Untitled, circa 1930
Gelatin silver print
23.1 x 16.5 cm — 9" x 6 1/2"
Jane Corkin Gallery, Toronto

Page 114 *Frédéric Mégret*, 1929
Gelatin silver print
9 x 11.2 cm — 3 1/2" x 4 1/2"
Man Ray Estate Settlement, 1994
Mnam/Cci, Centre Georges Pompidou
AM 1994-394/3250

Page 115 *Edward James*, 1937
Gelatin silver print
8.9 x 6.7 cm — 3 1/2" x 2 3/4"
Man Ray Estate Settlement, 1994
Mnam/Cci, Centre Georges Pompidou
AM 1994-394/781

Edward James, 1937
Gelatin silver print
9.3 x 6.3 cm — 3 3/4" x 2 1/2"
Man Ray Estate Settlement, 1994
Mnam/Cci, Centre Georges Pompidou
AM 1994-394/3818

Page 116 For Aragon's *Aurélien*, circa 1930
Gelatin silver print, printed and retouched
with pencil in the 1960s
Harry and Ann Malcolmson Collection,
Toronto

Page 117 *Jacqueline Goddard*, 1932
Solarized gelatin silver print
8.3 x 5.5 cm — 3 1/4" x 2 1/4"
Man Ray Estate Settlement, 1994
Mnam/Cci, Centre Georges Pompidou
AM 1994-394/2711

Page 118 *Tristan Tzara*, 1924
Gelatin silver contact print made from the
original negative by
Jacques Faujour and Daniel Valet in 1998
Man Ray Estate Settlement, 1994
Mnam/Cci, Centre Georges Pompidou

Study for the portrait of Tristan Tzara, 1921
Gelatin silver contact print made from the
original negative by
Jacques Faujour and Daniel Valet in 1998
Man Ray Estate Settlement, 1994
Mnam/Cci, Centre Georges Pompidou

Page 173 *Érotique Voilée*, 1933
Gelatin silver print
17.2 x 13 cm — 6 ³/4" x 5 ¹/4"
Private collection, Paris

Érotique Voilée, 1933
Gelatin silver print
12.1 x 9.1 cm — 4 ³/4" x 3 ¹/2"
Private collection, Paris

Page 174 Study for *Noire et Blanche*, 1926
Gelatin silver contact print made from the
original negative by
Jacques Faujour and Daniel Valet in 1998
Man Ray Estate Settlement, 1994
Mnam/Cci, Centre Georges Pompidou

Le Masque [The Mask], 1926
Gelatin silver print
10.5 x 7.4 cm — 4 ¹/4" x 3"
Collection Ken Browar, Paris

Page 175 *Noire et Blanche*, 1926
Gelatin silver print
23 x 17.5 cm — 9" x 7"
Mnam/Cci, Centre Georges Pompidou
AM 1987-885

Page 176 *"Drink to me only with ..."*, circa 1932
Gelatin silver print
7.6 x 5.2 cm — 3" x 2"
Man Ray Estate Settlement, 1994
Mnam/Cci, Centre Georges Pompidou
AM 1994-394/759

Page 177 Lydia and wooden figures, 1932
Gelatin silver print
8 x 9.8 cm — 3 ¹/4" x 3 ³/4"
Man Ray Estate Settlement, 1994
Mnam/Cci, Centre Georges Pompidou
1994-394/2277

Page 178 Lydia, study for *Les Larmes* [*Tears*], 1932
Gelatin silver print
8.5 x 5.7 cm — 3 ¹/4" x 2 ¹/4"
Man Ray Estate Settlement, 1994
Mnam/Cci, Centre Georges Pompidou
1994-394/3823

Lydia, study for *Les Larmes* [*Tears*], 1932
Gelatin silver print
8.3 x 5.6 cm — 3 ¹/4" x 2 ¹/4"
Man Ray Estate Settlement, 1994
Mnam/Cci, Centre Georges Pompidou
1994-394/2256

Page 179 *Les Larmes* [*Tears*], 1932
Gelatin silver print
16 x 23 cm — 6 ¹/4" x 9"
Bibliothèque Nationale de France, Paris

Les Larmes [*Tears*], 1932
Gelatin silver print
22.9 x 29.8 cm — 9" x 11 ³/4"
The J. Paul Getty Museum, Los Angeles

Page 180 Study for *L'Aurore des Objets*, 1937
Gelatin silver print
8.3 x 5.5 cm — 3 ¹/4" x 2 ¹/4"
Man Ray Estate Settlement, 1994
Mnam/Cci, Centre Georges Pompidou
AM 1994-394/4576

Page 181 Study for *L'Aurore des Objets*, 1937
Superimposition, gelatin silver print
8.5 x 5.5 cm — 3 ¹/4" x 2 ¹/4"
Man Ray Estate Settlement, 1994
Mnam/Cci, Centre Georges Pompidou
AM 1994-394/4574

L'Aurore des Objets, 1937
Gelatin silver print
23.2 x 18 cm — 9 ¹/4" x 7"
Mnam/Cci, Centre Georges Pompidou
AM 1982-167

Study for *L'Aurore des Objets*, 1937
Superimposition, gelatin silver print
8.3 x 5.8 cm — 3 ¹/4" x 2 ¹/4"
Man Ray Estate Settlement, 1994
Mnam/Cci, Centre Georges Pompidou
AM 1994-394/4571

Page 182 *Mains Peintes par Picasso* [Hands Painted by
Picasso], 1935
Gelatin silver print
8 x 10.5 cm — 3 ¹/4" x 4 ¹/4"
Man Ray Estate Settlement, 1994
Mnam/Cci, Centre Georges Pompidou
1994-394/2444

Page 183 Untitled, 1930
Gelatin silver print
29.2 x 22.1 cm — 11 ¹/2" x 8 ³/4"
The Museum of Modern Art, New York
Gift of James Thrall Soby

Page 184 Untitled, 1926
Gelatin silver print
22.7 x 29.5 cm — 9" x 11 ³/4"
The Museum of Modern Art, New York
Gift of James Thrall Soby

Page 185 Untitled, 1931
Solarized gelatin silver print
30 x 22 cm — 11 ³/4" x 8 ³/4"
Bibliothèque Nationale de France, Paris

Page 187 *Electricité*, 1931

Page 188 *Droller*, 1918
AM 1995-200 D

Page 189 *Der Sturm*, n°3, 1922

Page 190 Untitled, 1922
Rayograph, gelatin silver print
17.3 x 23.4 cm — 6 ³/4" x 9 ¹/4"
Private collection, Paris

Page 191 Untitled, 1922
Rayograph, gelatin silver print
17.5 x 23.4 cm — 7" x 9 ¹/4"
Private collection, Paris

Page 192 Untitled, 1923
Rayograph, gelatin silver print
The Museum of Modern Art, New York
Gift of James Thrall Soby

Page 195 Untitled, 1927
Rayograph, gelatin silver print
31 x 25 cm — 12 ¹/4" x 9 ³/4"
Manfred Heiting Collection, Amsterdam

Page 196 Untitled, 1943
Rayograph, gelatin silver print
35 x 27 cm — 13 ³/4" x 10 ³/4"
Private collection, Paris

Page 197 Untitled, 1925
Rayograph, gelatin silver print
23.8 x 18 cm — 9 ¹/2" x 7"
Manfred Heiting Collection, Amsterdam

Page 198 *Colifichet* [Frippery], 1923
Rayograph, gelatin silver print
29 x 23 cm — 11 ¹/2" x 9"
Sylvio Perlstein Collection, Antwerp

Page 199 Untitled, 1924
Rayograph, gelatin silver print
39.9 x 29.8 cm — 15 ³/4" x 11 ³/4"
The J. Paul Getty Museum, Los Angeles

Page 200 Untitled, 1945
Rayograph, gelatin silver print
36 x 28 cm — 14 ¹/4" x 11"
Sylvio Perlstein Collection, Antwerp

Page 201 Untitled, 1923
Rayograph, gelatin silver print
24.1 x 16.5 cm — 9 ¹/2" x 6 ¹/2"
The Art Institute of Chicago, Julien Levy
Collection
Special Photography Acquisition Fund,
1979.97

Page 202 Untitled, 1945
Rayograph, gelatin silver print
35.2 x 27.5 cm — 13 ³/4" x 10 ³/4"
The Art Institute of Chicago,
Restricted gift of Miss Margaret Fisher,
1973.255

Page 203 Untitled, 1923
Rayograph, gelatin silver print
29.7 x 24 cm — 11" x 9 ¹/2"
The J. Paul Getty Museum, Los Angeles

Page 204 Untitled, 1923
Rayograph, gelatin silver print
23.9 x 17.8 cm — 9 ¹/2" x 7"
The Museum of Modern Art, New York
Purchase

Page 205 Untitled, 1922
Rayograph, gelatin silver print
23.9 x 30 cm — 9 ¹/2" x 11 ³/4"
The Museum of Modern Art, New York
Gift of James Thrall Soby

Page 206 *Head, New York*, 1920
Gelatin silver print
22.3 x 16.8 cm — 8 ³/4" x 6 ³/4"
The J. Paul Getty Museum, Los Angeles

Page 208 *Integration of Shadows*, 1919
Gelatin silver print
23.9 x 17.6 cm — 9 ¹/2" x 7"
Mnam/Cci, Centre Georges Pompidou
AM 1982-177

L'Homme, 1920
Gelatin silver print
39 x 29 cm — 15 ¹/4" x 11 ¹/2"
Fondazione Marguerite Arp, Locarno

Page 209 *La Femme*, 1920
Gelatin silver print
38.8 x 29.1 cm — 15 ¹/4" x 11 ¹/2"
Mnam/Cci, Centre Georges Pompidou
AM 1973-23

Page 210 *Coat Stand*, 1920
Gelatin silver print
41 x 28.6 cm — 16 1/4" x 11 1/4"
Mnam/Cci, Centre Georges Pompidou
AM 1996-217

Page 212 Marcel Duchamp, Bonds for Monte-Carlo roulette, 1924
Gelatin silver print
8.9 x 11.9 cm — 3 1/2" x 4 3/4"
Man Ray Estate Settlement, 1994
Mnam/Cci, Centre Georges Pompidou
AM 1994-394/2319

Marcel Duchamp, Bonds for Monte-Carlo roulette, 1924
Gelatin silver print
9 x 11.9 cm — 3 1/2" x 4 3/4"
Man Ray Estate Settlement, 1994
Mnam/Cci, Centre Georges Pompidou
AM 1994-394/2318

Page 215 *Joseph Stella and Marcel Duchamp*
Gelatin silver print
20.5 x 15.6 cm — 8" x 6 1/4"
The J. Paul Getty Museum, Los Angeles

Page 217 *Transatlantic*, 1921
Gelatin silver print, collage, paint on wood
36.7 x 24.8 cm — 14 1/2" x 13 3/4"
Jedermann Collection N.A., New York

Page 218 *Collection d'Hiver* [Winter Collection], 1936
Gelatin silver print
35 x 24.1 cm — 13 3/4" x 9 1/2"
Private collection, Paris

Page 219 *Enough Rope*, 1944
Gelatin silver print
25.8 x 20 cm — 10 1/4" x 8"
Private collection, Paris

Page 220 *Le Bouquet*, 1935
Gelatin silver print
28.9 x 23 cm — 11 1/2" x 9"
Private collection, Morges

Page 221 *Feu_d'Artifice* [Fireworks], 1934
Gelatin silver print
29.2 x 22.5 cm — 11 1/2" x 8 3/4"
Mnam/Cci, Centre Georges Pompidou
AM 1982-169

Page 222 *Lee Miller*, circa 1930
Gelatin silver print
22.9 x 17.7 cm — 9" x 7"
Lee Miller Archives, Great Britain

Page 223 Silhouette, 1930
Gelatin silver print
29.3 x 22.5 cm — 11 1/2" x 8 3/4"
The Museum of Modern Art, New York
Gift of James Thrall Soby

Page 224 *Anatomies*, 1929
Gelatin silver print
22.6 x 17.2 cm — 9" x 6 3/4"
The Museum of Modern Art, New York
Gift of James Thrall Soby

Page 225 Untitled, 1933
Gelatin silver print
17.9 x 21.3 cm — 7" x 8 1/2"
Private collection, Geneva

Untitled, 1933
Gelatin silver print
17.2 x 13.4 cm — 6 3/4" x 5 1/4"
Private collection, Geneva

226 / 227 *Minotaure*, 1933
Gelatin silver print
15 x 23.3 cm — 6" x 9 1/4"
Michael Senft, Jack Banning, New York

Page 228 *Explosante-fixe*, 1934
Gelatin silver print
22.8 x 17.8 cm — 9" x 7"
Private collection, Paris. Courtesy Galerie 1900*2000

Page 229 Prou del Pilar, study for *Explosante-fixe*, 1934
Gelatin silver print
10.7 x 7.8 cm — 6 3/4" x 3"
Man Ray Estate Settlement, 1994
Mnam/Cci, Centre Georges Pompidou
AM 1994-394/883

Prou del Pilar, study for *Explosante-fixe*, 1934
Gelatin silver print
10.7 x 7.8 cm — 4 1/4" x 3"
Man Ray Estate Settlement, 1994
Mnam/Cci, Centre Georges Pompidou
AM 1994-394/882

Page 230 Untitled, 1924
Gelatin silver print
16 x 11.5 cm — 6 1/4" x 4 1/2"
Courtesy Alain Paviot, Paris

Page 231 *Élevage de Poussière* [Dust Breeding], 1920
Gelatin silver print
11.4 x 17.2 cm — 4 1/2" x 6 3/4"
Manfred Heiting, Amsterdam

Page 232 *Course d'Autos* [Car Race], 1926
Gelatin silver print
8.9 x 11.9 cm — 3 1/2" x 4 3/4"
Timothy Baum Collection, New York

Page 233 *Contacts For Shakespearian [Sic],Equations*, 1935-1948
Album (10 pages), 31 contact prints glued to paper
21.6 x 14.1 cm — 8 1/2" x 5 1/2"
Man Ray Estate Settlement, 1994
Mnam/Cci, Centre Georges Pompidou
AM 1994-392

Page 234 *Objet Mathématique* [Mathematical Object], 1934-1936
Gelatin silver print
24 x 30 cm — 8 1/2" x 11 3/4"
Man Ray Estate Settlement, 1994
Mnam/Cci, Centre Georges Pompidou
AM 1994-391 (3)

Page 235 *Objet Mathématique* [Mathematical Object], 1934-1936
Gelatin silver print
24 x 30 cm — 9 1/2" x 11 3/4"
Man Ray Estate Settlement, 1994
Mnam/Cci, Centre Georges Pompidou
AM 1994-391 (2)

Page 236 *Marcel Duchamp*, Distorsion [Marcel Duchamp Distorted], 1925
Gelatin silver print
12.6 x 8.8 cm — 5" x 3 1/2"
Private collection, Paris

Page 237 *Moving Sculpture* or *La France*, 1920
Gelatin silver print
7.5 x 12 cm — 3" x 4 3/4"
Jedermann Collection N.A., New York

Page 238 Portrait, circa 1930
Gelatin silver print
12.2 x 17.2 cm — 4 3/4" x 6 3/4"
Man Ray Estate Settlement, 1994
Mnam/Cci, Centre Georges Pompidou
AM 1994-394/547

Untitled, circa 1930
Superimposition, gelatin silver print
13 x 17.8 cm — 5 1/4" x 7"
Private collection, Paris

Page 239 *Marcel Duchamp*, circa 1920
Superimposition, gelatin silver print
17.9 x 12.8 cm — 7" x 5"
Private collection, Paris

Page 258 *Homme d'Affaires* [*Businessman*], 1926
Gelatin silver print
4.4 x 5.7 cm — 1 3/4" x 2 1/4"
Man Ray Estate Settlement, 1994
Mnam/Cci, Centre Georges Pompidou
1994-394/1002

Homme d'Affaires [*Businessman*], 1926
Gelatin silver print
4.4 x 5.6 cm — 1 3/4" x 2 1/4"
Man Ray Estate Settlement, 1994
Mnam/Cci, Centre Georges Pompidou
AM 1994-394/1003

Homme d'Affaires [*Businessman*], 1926
Gelatin silver print
4.4 x 5.8 cm — 1 3/4" x 2 1/4"
Man Ray Estate Settlement, 1994
Mnam/Cci, Centre Georges Pompidou
1994-394/1005

Page 259 *Homme d'Affaires* [*Businessman*], 1926
Gelatin silver print
4.4 x 5.8 cm — 1 3/4" x 2 1/4"
Man Ray Estate Settlement, 1994
Mnam/Cci, Centre Georges Pompidou
1994-394/1007

Homme d'Affaires [*Businessman*], 1926
Gelatin silver print
4.4 x 5.9 cm — 1 3/4" x 2 1/4"
Man Ray Estate Settlement, 1994
Mnam/Cci, Centre Georges Pompidou
1994-394/997

Homme d'Affaires [*Businessman*], 1926
Gelatin silver print
4.4 x 5.9 cm — 1 3/4" x 2 1/4"
Man Ray Estate Settlement, 1994
Mnam/Cci, Centre Georges Pompidou
1994-394/1000

Note on titles :

"Official" titles, whether assigned by Man Ray himself or acquired by tradition, are given here in italics, whereas unofficial titles remain in roman typeface. The same distinction holds for the English versions of French titles, given in brackets. By convention, certain French titles are generally employed in English rather than translated
(*Noire et Blanche*, *Violon d'Ingres*).

Homme d'Affaires [*Businessman*], 1926

Photograph Credits